more food of my friends:

their favorite recipes

Other books by Judith Shepard

SEASCAPES

FOOD OF MY FRIENDS

judith shepard

more food of my friends:
their favorite recipes

the permanent press
sag harbor, n.y. 11963

Library of Congress Number: 82-084010.
International Standard Book Number: 0-932966-29-2.
Manufactured in the United States of America
Typography by Raven Type, Charlotte, N.C.
THE PERMANENT PRESS
Sagaponack NY 11962

thanks

To all cooks everywhere and especially to those who contributed so enthusiastically to this book.
To Karen Sukoneck, who again designed such a nice cover.
To Mary Cummings, who again edited for me.
To my husband, Marty, who somehow gets it all together and who loves to test the recipes.

contents

foreword

In 1981, I wrote a cookbook called *Food Of My Friends-The Best Meals in Town*. It came about because of a remark my husband Marty made. He said that he was spoiled. He didn't like to eat in restaurants anymore because "our home and the homes of our friends served the best meals in town." My book was, as the title implies, a collection of recipes from my friends as well as some of my own.

When I decided to write a second cookbook, I thought it would be a little more difficult and would take much longer to gather a sufficient number of dishes. I felt I might have exhausted my own supply and I would have to find more friends, relatives and even strangers who would be willing to share their favorite recipes. I was wrong. People were so willing to make contributions and were so helpful and supportive that this became the easiest part of the book.

I had a grand time. It was quite exciting to be given a recipe and then test it out on my family, definitely another bonus for writing a book like this. It made mealtime a bit of an adventure.

And the recipes came from all over. Some of my friends invented new ones especially for this book and I was inspired to create some myself — I who usually consider myself a recipe follower. Even my husband joined in by creating his own pasta sauce.

Other people dug up old family recipes. I found some of mine that were written on paper so old and yellow that it practically disintegrated before my eyes.

My mother gave me one that had been my grandmother's. It became a favorite of mine. I passed it on to my daughter, Liza, and now there will have been three generations of us preparing "Quilting Bees."

Everyone seemed to be on the lookout for me. Gay Tarlo came back from a party in New York City and called to tell me about a chicken salad she had enjoyed so much that she jotted down the ingredients so I could include it here. An acquaintance who lives on a commune sent me a whole sheaf of recipes telling me to use whatever I wanted. Franklin Heller wrote a P.S. on the bottom of a business letter asking if I would like an old family recipe for Liptaur Cheese which I eagerly accepted.

I think I am the most partial to family recipes, the ones that have been handed down. It may be only an illusion, of course, but it speaks of a kind of continuity that is very appealing to me. And if they weren't family recipes, I liked the idea that people were so eager to share. After all, it doesn't cost anything and it contributes to a whole culinary network — a cultural menu of our times, if you will.

So, I consider this book first of all a collaborative effort and an indication of the essential willingness of people to share something that gives us all pleasure.

Judith Shepard
Sag Harbor, N.Y.

introduction

About 19 years ago, I picked up a book by Gaylord Hauser which changed my ideas about food and nutrition and set me upon a path that I am still trying to follow. Mr. Hauser talked about being attentive to what you eat and how you prepare it, and about the benefits this can bring for your health and general well being. It made a lot of sense to me then and does even more so now that my knowledge and experience in this subject has increased.

At the time, my ex-husband and I were traveling across country in a play called "Who's Afraid of Virginia Wolfe?." The tour was ten months long; we had our three children, Aaron, Liza, and Caleb with us, all of whom were under five, and anything that I could do to make this venture easier and less fatiguing was very welcome. After reading Mr. Hauser's book, I became excited by the idea that I might have some measure of control over my family's health and, of course, my own. I began changing some of my cooking concepts and trying Mr. Hauser's recipes. When I began to notice a definite change in our physical and mental state, I became a true convert.

At that time, people were not nearly as health and diet-conscious as they are now. In fact, certain ideas that are quite germaine to sound nutrition now might have been denounced as fads then. I find the whole emphasis and investigation into the importance of eating wisely, by both laymen and the medical community, a welcome sign of progress.

I also find that I continue to change and refine my thinking on this subject as I become older. I have watched my friends change as they modify their diets. It's not unusual to be invited to a dinner party and have the hostess announce that she has been cooking without much salt and that there is a salt shaker on the table for those who might want to add more. More and more people either don't allow smoking in their homes or set aside a separate room for smokers. And, while this is not an exercise book, I would point out that, for many of us, diet has gone hand-in-hand with exercise. Just as people have become more aware of good nutrition, they have also realized the importance of keeping their bodies in good shape.

I continue to be appalled at the way food is manipulated for a longer shelf life and more profit. The preservatives, additives, bleaches, emulsifiers, mono and diglycerides, other chemicals, and vast amounts of sugar and salt are not for me. I feel it is up to us, the consumers, to show that we will not be force fed these inferior foods and we should refuse to buy such products. If enough people boycott these items, maybe those who are responsible for producing them will be reeducated. It is our health that counts, not their profits.

I do have a fair number of recipes in my book calling for meat. I also have some rich and luscious desserts and recipes that do not adhere to strict dietary rules. Since many of these contributions are very tasty, I have included them. What I do strive for, however, is some kind of balance. I don't make them too often. I try to stick to main courses of vegetables, poultry or fish, salads, fruits, and simple desserts. However, I do eat meat and rich dishes and desserts occasionally. As I said in first cookbook, "Everything in moderation, including moderation."

One of the newer things I am working on these days is improving the appearance of the food when it reaches the table. One only has to think about Japanese dishes or look through some of the cookbooks that have expensive, glossy pictures to see what I mean. They practically make your mouth water. I am convinced that to see a beautifully laid table with balanced colors and textures must do something for one's psyche. Since I like the ritual of dining with all that it implies — the sharing of ideas, the coming together at a certain time of day or evening — setting an attractive table seems like a necessary component.

I am also trying to strike a balance between rich and lean, piquant and bland, solid and liquid when preparing menus. Of course, weather plays a part too. A chilled fruit soup is superb during a hot summer evening, but is not so desirable in December. Hearty stews and black bread are great during blizzards, but not during a muggy July evening. So it's worthwhile and rather intriguing to let the weather help you plan your menu and to see where your creativity might lead you.

One last thing concerns the people who have contributed these recipes. Half the fun of writing my first book was that I could write a little bit about my friends. Since many of the same people have contributed recipes for this book too, I hope they will understand that I didn't want to repeat myself. My new contributors I have described briefly. I guess it's a way of sharing and spreading our community to other places and people. I hope that any of the recipes that especially please you will be passed along too.

notes and guidelines

notes and guidelines

This may be somewhat repetitious for those of you who have read my first book, but I feel that there are some basic rules that one should be aware of in planning meals. Most of the information I'm passing on has come from various books and sources that I have read over the years, starting from the first one by Gaylord Hauser, on to Adele Davis, and more recently the New York Times which cited a report by an expert panel of the National Academy of Sciences in which the kind of dietary recommendations that so-called food faddists have been advocating for years are confirmed. Many well informed people, very concerned with the relationship between diet and health, have been treated with a certain derision by the scientific and medical community. Now it is beginning to look as though that community is catching up with them. And I hope new doctors and nurses in training are beginning to take diet and food intake very seriously, so we all can begin to practice preventive health. Preventive health is a silly way of putting it since, after all, what we want is to prevent sickness before it happens. However, it is the term that both doctors and dentists seem to be using. There are many fine source books that you can read if you would like more comprehensive information than what I am giving you in this book.

My own notes and guidelines change as new information becomes available. A few years ago, I tried cutting down on my salt intake; now I cut down even more. My menu planning becomes more selective and I see the same thing occurring with my friends. We are all watching our weight more carefully. Fewer and fewer of us are serving lots of cheeses with cocktails. Rich pastries are being replaced with light desserts.

I have mentioned that I am not a purist, so I try to be somewhat flexible while not indulging myself too much. Although a Pavlova is an exquisite dessert, I serve it only on special occasions. I dearly love all kinds of pasta, but I am not going to make all those dishes that contain huge amounts of butter and cream too often.

I hope that you will follow some of these guidelines while realizing that knowledge about food, its preparation and its effects on health is always evolving. People talk about adventures in good eating; they could also talk about adventures in good health.

1. Shopping

My first rule of thumb is to shop for quality. I would rather have less of a good thing than more of a bad thing. I would rather have a smaller cut of prime meat and have it less often. I would rather buy good, fresh fish a couple of times a month than any of the frozen fish found in supermarkets. I try to buy vegetables and fruits in season and when that's not possible, I still look for the best quality.

I believe that it is important to find a good butcher, fishmonger and green grocer. They can be your best friends. It is true that it is very convenient to buy all your foods at one market. Unfortunately, it seems that the quality of certain foods just won't be as good. To travel to those shopkeepers who offer the highest quality takes a certain degree of organization and a desire to buy only the best. I try to stay away from canned and frozen foods as much as possible. Fresh fruits and vegetables simply taste better and they're better for you.

I do not buy convenience foods. As far as I'm concerned, they're only convenient for the manufacturer; they usually taste awful and cost much more than they're worth.

So, shop in season, shop for quality, and find good sources for your food.

2. Meat

The panel of the National Academy of Sciences has advised Americans to eat less fat and very little salt-cured, pickled and smoked foods. Try to cut down your meat intake. We have meat a couple of times a month and then I try to find the leanest pieces I can. Try not to buy meat that contains nitrates and nitrites. Don't buy smoked meat or fish. They are all said to contain cancer causing substances. We never eat ham, but once in a while I indulge and buy bacon. If you look hard, you can find bacon and hotdogs that do not contain nitrates and nitrites. Try to wean yourself to fish and poultry. It's not as hard as it may seem.

3. Additives

I don't buy anything that contains additives, preservatives, artificial colors and dyes, calcium proprionate, dough conditioners, (which may contain sodium stearoyl-2 lactylate, mono and diglycerides, ethoxylated mono and diglycerides, and succinylated mono glycerides). I don't buy breads that contain yeast conditioners. It may sound innocuous, but yeast conditioners are ammonium chloride and potassium bromate and, who needs that in his bread? If a bread says, "no preservatives," look very carefully because chances are it has something in it that shouldn't be there. All this means that you must read your labels each time. The manufacturers do try to fool you.

It may also mean that you might want to start baking your own bread because good healthy breads are hard to find. Recently, I heard a doctor who had been given a great deal of recognition for his study on cancer viruses. He said that if there were one thing that he would like to tell the American public about their health it was this: Eat more bread, but good healthy bread, bread made with unbleached, stoneground flours, flours with bran and wheat germ — the kind of bread your grandmother probably made.

4. Butter, Oils, and Margarines

I am aware of the dilemma over choosing between butter and margarine. Butter is saturated fat and the less we have of it, the better. Margarines, on the other hand, usually are unsaturated fats, but they contain additives and food dyes. In the past I have opted for sweet butter. The salt in salted butters can mask rancidity and I don't want that extra salt anyway. However, now I have come upon a new variation — a combination of butter and safflower oil that you blend yourself. It has the advantage of having less saturated fat and spreading like margarine without the harmful additives. I am very pleased to have this substitute, my family likes it, and it is easy to prepare. I call it butterblend for want of a proper name, and I have included the recipe (page 29).

I try to substitute vegetable oils for butter whenever I can. However, hydrogenated oils contain preservatives to increase their shelf life. Some vegetable oils contain cottonseed oil. Cotton is not considered an edible crop and is heavily sprayed with pesticides which I'm sure make their way into the oil so, here again, you must read your labels carefully.

My favorite oil is a cold-pressed poly-unsaturated safflower oil. It's light and can be used for salads, sauteíng and dishes cooked in a wok. I occasionally use olive, sesame and walnut oils.

In cutting down one's use of oil, I find if you use heavy pans and let them get quite hot, you can reduce the amount of oil. Use a rubber spatula to see that the whole surface is lubricated.

5. Sweeteners

I don't use white sugar. It has been sneaked in so many foods that probably I'm getting a lot of it anyway. It causes obesity, tooth decay, and depletes B vitamins in the body. Raw sugar is not too much better, but I use it when I need to because at least it hasn't gone through the refining process, and it may contain some of the original nutrients. Chemicals have not been added to make it anti-caking and it hasn't been exposed to the whitening process.

The best sugar substitutes are honey, molasses and maple syrup. Maple syrup should be pure and unrefined. The commercial brands contain artificial flavor, sodium benzoate and sorbic acid.

6. Flour

If I have to use white flour, I make sure it's unbleached. I do try to use stoneground, unrefined whole wheat flour as much as possible or at least a combination of whole wheat and white flours. Whole wheat flour can certainly be used for thickening sauces and gravies. It makes delicious breads and muffins and is one of the best ways to include more of the nutrients we need for good health. Desserts made with whole wheat flour can be a little heavy so I often try to use a combination of unbleached white and whole wheat flours. Stay away from flours that have been bromated or phosphated.

7. Rice

I like both brown and white rice, but brown rice is better for you. It contains all the natural ingredients many of which white rice loses in the processing. When I do use white rice, I choose the converted brands because they may contain some of the original nutrients. I never buy quick-cooking or seasoned rice. Quick-cooking rice contains chemicals which have been added to reduce to cooking time; seasoned rice is replete with additives.

8. Grains, Beans and So Forth

I am trying to become more knowledgeable about the various grains available to us. Rice is only one of them. Others include cracked wheat, kasha, barley, millet, corn meal, lentils, wild rice, rye and hominy. There seems to be a tremendous variety of recipes using these ingredients and I'm sure eating more of them could do much to improve our diets. In the back I've listed some of my favorite cookbooks. Two of them, "Whole Grain Cookery" by Stella Standard and "Future Foods" by Colin Tudge should give all of us enough recipes to experiment with for two lifetimes. There are too many nutritious foodstuffs to restrict ourselves to just rice, noodles and potatoes.

9. Milk, Cream, Yogurt and Cheese

High fat dairy products are simply not that good for you. It is very hard for me to cut down on cheese and I love cream. One of the ways I try to compensate is by using dry, skim milk. Whenever a recipe calls for milk, you can simply mix dry milk with the prescribed amount of water and use that as a substitute. You can make skim milk and mix it half and half with regular milk for drinking and you can make yogurt with any kind of substitution. You can even make it with all skim milk. In this way, you not only are saving money, but you are cutting down on dairy fats.

In buying yogurt, beware of those that contain fruit. They usually contain incredible amounts of sugar. It's better to buy the plain kind and mix it with fresh fruit.

When buying cheeses, check for additives. Because all ingredients are not labeled, I often buy imported kinds. Since some countries are very proud of their cheeses, they often do not add preservatives, not wanting to tamper with a good thing.

10. Breakfast Cereals

This year I have been trying to use a variety of both hot and cold breakfast cereals. I seldom buy cold cereals in supermarkets because they are usually quite dreadful and loaded with sugar. I either make my own or buy them at my local health food store. When buying cereals, you must read all the labels very carefully.

Some of the hot cereals you might try besides oatmeal and cream of wheat are kasha, cream of rice, wheatena, cornmeal, cracked wheat, cream of rye, and whole wheat cereal.

Do not buy quick cooking cereals because they have been over processed.

I also try to add untoasted wheatgerm to both hot and cold cereals because it is so high in nutrients. Keep it in the refrigerator so that it does not spoil and become rancid.

11. Salt

I think everyone knows these days that we consume far too much salt and that it is not good for you in such quantities. It is a natural ingredient in all foods, but has been added by the food industry in overwhelming amounts. I have listed the standard "salt and pepper" in many of my recipes but I have not given the amounts, preferring to leave that to individual tastes. However, more and more, I find myself eliminating the salt entirely. For those of us who use tamari (soy sauce) as a substitute, I must add that it is also loaded with salt. When I do use salt, I buy vegetable or sea salt. Too many of the salts sold in supermarkets have many additives, including aluminum compounds and agents to make the salt pour easily.

One final word — I think we have become addicted to salt and also sugar. As with all addictions, it is hard to cut down or eliminate them. But I do believe if you stick with it, you become more appreciative of the taste of the food itself and that idea may help you when you automatically reach for the salt shaker or find yourself starting to add an extra teaspoon of sugar.

12. Health Food Supplies

Many supermarkets now carry health foods and have special sections allotted to those products. I think they are worth looking into and one should also find a convenient health food store. As people have become more and more conscious of the quality of the food they buy, health food sections have expanded and today you can find many different kinds of flour, breakfast cereals, unsulphured dried fruits, good selections of tamari, nut butters, bouillon cubes, crackers, juices without added sugar, and even hot dogs and bacon preserved without nitrates and nitrites. Some are exorbitantly priced, so you must be knowledgeable and shop wisely. Be aware that these items do not have preservatives and many must be refrigerated. Since some of these products cost more than the usual supermarket variety, you may have to be a more skillful juggler with your food budget.

13. Cooking Methods

I try to steam vegetables or at least to use as little water as possible. I like to prepare dishes in a wok. Baking is preferable to frying and, when I do fry or saute, I cheat a little and use less oil than is called for. I seldom deep fry, although once in a while, as with tempura, there is no way to get around it.

A good set of pots and pans is a wise investment. I do not use teflon or aluminum pans as they are made with soft materials that can dissolve and be ingested. Stainless steel, heavy cast iron or clay pots seem to be the best.

14. Quantity

Most of the recipes in this book serve four to six people.

15. Time and Procedures

Good healthful cooking takes more time; there's no doubt about it. It's a choice you have to make. Sometimes, I find that I have overdone it. I am so busy preparing meals that I don't have time to do anything else. I am solving this dilemma by more careful planning. If I am having a dinner that takes quite a lot of time, lunch must be simple. If I make enchiladas for dinner, the accompaniments must take only moments to prepare. If I decide to bake bread, maybe I can get my husband to cook something for dinner. For if I'm not careful, I am like the child whose eyes are too big for her stomach, only I am the cook who has such wonderful fantasies of all the delectable things I'm going to make, that I am literally a slave to my kitchen.

In order to make planning easier, I have starred every recipe. One star represents a dish that is easy or quick to prepare, a recipe with two stars takes more time, and three stars tells you that this is something that requires longer preparation.

It is very useful to read the recipe all the way through before you begin. This way, you won't be caught without one of the ingredients or find at the end that the dish is supposed to marinate overnight.

A lot of the best cooks I know all have the same habit. They taste as they go along, so it seems to me that it would be well to adopt this practice.

Last but not least, cooking is a creative act. It helps to think of it that way, especially since it's something many of us must do every day. If it is done with a sense of adventure, if you delight in tempting the senses, and if you think of yourself as an artist, you will be well rewarded by friends and family, and what is a chore for many, will be a pleasure for you.

Hints

These are a few hints that you might want to glance through. I have jotted them down as I have written this book as experience has taught me that they are easy and very useful.

1. Fresh herbs and spices are always preferable to dried ones, when available.
2. My Italian food store sells me chunks of Romano cheese instead of Parmesan and the owner, Savario, says it is fine in Italian dishes and much less expensive.
3. I prefer to cook my pasta *al dente* which means that it is a tiny bit firm. Otherwise, by the time you get it to the table, the pasta is too mushy.
4. I see no reason to add salt to all boiling water, such as that for vegetables and pasta. People can always add more at the table.
5. Mushrooms absorb water easily, so they should be cleaned with a damp cloth.
6. Many dishes that have tomatoes will taste better if the sauce is well cooked down, especially pasta sauces. If you wish, you can drain the tomatoes before adding them. The point is to have a rich, thick sauce, not a watery one. Save the liquid for a soup. I might add that when I make a tomato sauce for pasta dishes, it it's summer and fresh tomatoes are plentiful and inexpensive, I use them skinned and chopped as a substitute for canned tomatoes. Because tomatoes *are* so watery, I like to toss a salad first and add them at the last moment.
7. When you are cooking a delicate fish, be sure you have plenty of room in the pan so you are able to turn the fillets easily. Otherwise, they will flake apart.
8. All roasts should stand 10 to 15 minutes before carving for easier slicing and juicier meat.
9. I have a standard rule for tossing salads (when you are not using a mixed dressing)-. Always toss the leaves with the oil first. This way the leaves are well coated before the vinegar or lemon juice is added.
10. It is very difficult to find a good cream that does not contain stabilizers and emulsifiers. If you find one, make a note of it and don't settle for anything else.
11. Mix dry milk with the prescribed amount of water to substitute for regular milk in all baking.
12. Eggplant soaks up enormous amounts of oil. When a recipe calls for sauteed or fried eggplant, try putting the slices in a well oiled baking dish to brown. They should occasionally be turned.
13. When a recipe calls for stir frying, you don't have to go through all your Chinese cookbooks or take a cooking class. It simply means to cook food that has been cut up in a large wok or frying pan in a small amount of oil over high heat. As it cooks, keep flipping the pieces over and over using two utensils until they are cooked or coated as the recipe requires.
14. Bouillon cubes should definitely be purchased in health food stores. Otherwise, you are getting pure salt and chemicals.
15. Prepare fish the same day it is caught or bought. It should not have any kind of a fishy smell.

16. Store brown sugar in a jar with a lid and include a small piece of apple to prevent the sugar from hardening.
17. Generally speaking, use a third or a half as much of dried herbs as you would if they were fresh and buy both kinds in small quantities as they lose their delicate flavor quickly.
18. Store soups that have been made with meat or poultry in the refrigerator so that you are able to skim off the grease easily before heating and serving.
19. It is nice to be able to store pie crusts in your freezer in case you want to make a quick quiche or fruit pie. If you don't want to make your own there are some frozen brands available with pure ingredients, so look for those.

appetizers and side dishes

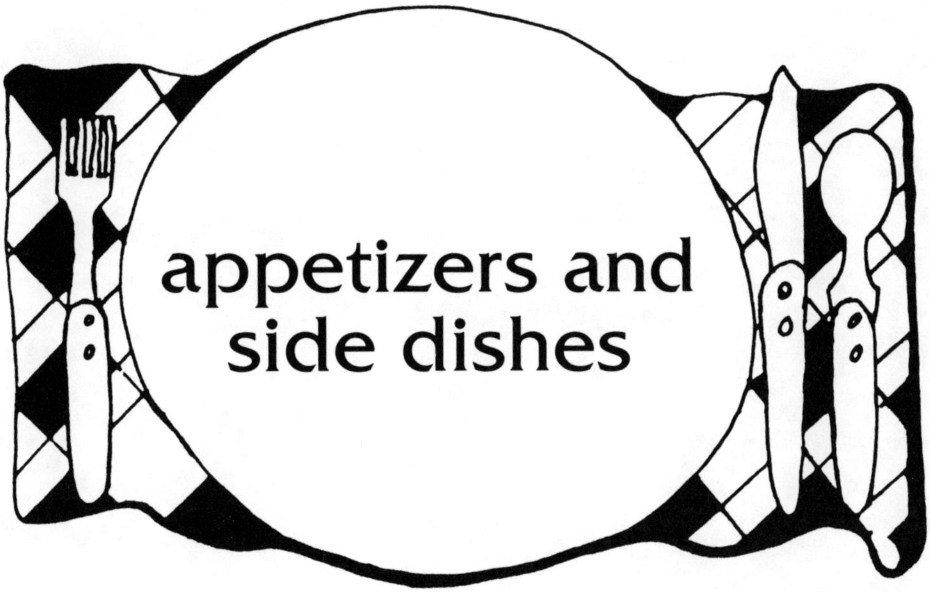

My good friend, Bill Tarlo, is a fine creative cook, blending and tasting as he goes along. He is especially creative at artful combinations, as you can see by this invention. This is easy and quick to prepare. You can substitute yogurt for sour cream, if you're counting calories.

bill tarlo's cabbage & beet appetizer *

- 1 16 oz. jar beets, drained
- 1 16 oz. jar red cabbage, drained
- ¾ cup sour cream
- 3 tbsp. orange juice

1. Mix all ingredients together and serve as a side dish or even as a salad.

My husband said I should put this in my cookbook. I had never thought of it; it seemed so simple. This is what most of the Greek women who lived in my neighborhood in Silver Spring, Md. did with olives. I know you can buy them at delicatessens, but there's something nice about making your own. The longer they marinate, the better they'll be. I happen to like the olives with pits, but you can use pitted ones, if you wish.

greek olives *

- 3 cups black or green olives
- 1 cup olive oil
- ½ cup wine vinegar
- 2 cloves garlic
- 1 bay leaf
- 1 tsp. oregano

1. Make a small cut in each of the olives.
2. Put olives in a jar with a top and cover with all the rest of the ingredients.
3. Store in refrigerator.

Franklin Heller says that this is an old Viennese recipe passed down to them and that the trick is the crushed caraway seeds. However, that's very hard to do. I believe they can be purchased in some specialty shops. I used regular seeds and found it perfectly acceptable. I also think it's absolutely delicious.

franklin and banne heller's liptauer cheese spread *

- 2 8 oz. packages cream cheese
- 1 4 oz. stick butter
- 1 tbsp. caraway seeds, crushed if possible
- 1 tbsp. paprika
- 1 tbsp. prepared mustard
- ½ tsp. white pepper
- ¼ tsp. salt
- 2 anchovies minced (optional)
- 2 tbsp. capers, chopped
- 3 tbsp. fresh chives, chopped
- 1 tsp. fresh dill, chopped
- 2 tbsp. gin or brandy

1. Allow cream cheese and butter to soften and then mix together.
2. Add all the other ingredients and blend thoroughly.
3. Put in a container filled to the top and cover tightly.
4. Refrigerate for three days before serving.
5. When serving, use at room temperature with crackers or sliced pumpernickel.

This was a dip served to us at Cynthia Epstein's house. She is my husband's cousin, a marvelous cook in her own right. However, this was made by one of her house guests who gives cooking classes in New York City. I like it because it gives you another way to use tahini (sesame butter).

eggplant tahini dip *

- 1 eggplant, steamed
- 3 tsp. tahini
- 2 tsp. olive oil
- ¼ cup onion, minced
- 2 garlic cloves, pressed
- salt & pepper
- juice from 1 lemon
- 2 tbsp. parsley, minced

1. Peel eggplant, chop it very well and let it drain in a colander. Remove.
2. Add tahini and olive oil and mix well.
3. Add onion, garlic, salt and pepper and stir.
4. Add the lemon juice, stir again and sprinkle parsley on top.
5. Serve with crackers.

My friend Ginger showed me how to make a nice simple chutney. It's less expensive than buying it and goes well with not only curries, but all kinds of roasts and vegetarian meals.

ginger's orange chutney *

1 18-oz. jar orange marmalade
¼ cup green pepper, seeded and chopped in small pieces
¼ cup onions, chopped fine
1 large apple, peeled, seeded and chopped
¼ cup raisins
1 tbsp. cider vinegar
dash of cayenne pepper

1. Mix all ingredients together and store in refrigerator until ready to serve.

bernice hunt's caviar pie **

This is an elegant, very easy, very impressive appetizer.

8 hardboiled eggs
1 small onion, chopped fine
salt and pepper
mayonnaise
3-4 tbsp. sour cream
8 ounces cream cheese, room temperature
3-4 ounces black caviar

1. Make a hardboiled egg salad by mashing the eggs with finely chopped onion, salt and pepper to taste, and just enough mayonnaise to hold the mixture together. (You can make it quickly in a food processor.)
2. Spread the egg salad evenly over the bottom of an 8- or 9-inch springform. Blend enough sour cream into the cream cheese to make it easily spreadable (use the processor again) and distribute it evenly over the egg mixture. Cover with plastic wrap and refrigerate until just before serving. (You can do this much the day before.)
3. Run a knife around the rim of the springform and remove it. Leave the pie on the base of the pan but set it on a large plate. Cover the top of the pie with a layer of caviar and place a wreath of watercress or parsley around the edge of the plate.
4. Serve with melba toast or small slices of French bread. Enough for at least 12 people.

Ruth and Arthur Steel are childhood sweethearts who have been happily enjoying each other for over 40 years. They live on the ocean in Bridgehampton and seem to be ready to experience just about anything from dancing at the local discotheque to embarking on a camel ride through Turkey. Attractive, well informed, and energetic, they entertain graciously and easily. I buy an inexpensive caviar from the local supermarket for this spread of Ruth's.

ruth steel's caviar spread *

1 cup whipped cream cheese
2 tbsp. minced onion
3 tbsp. lemon juice
8 tsp. black caviar

1. Mix the first three ingredients.
2. Fold the caviar in gently and serve immediately with melba toast or crackers.

pickled carrot sticks *

4 good sized carrots
1 large garlic clove, sliced
½ tsp. red pepper flakes
3 peppercorns
½ tsp. dry mustard
2 slices of fresh ginger about the size of a dime.
¼ cup apple cider vinegar

1. Slice carrots in julienne strips.
2. Place in bowl with all the rest of the ingredients and marinate overnight.

Kathy Fisher is a potter and makes beautiful tiles. One night she brought this spread to one of our communal meals and it was gone in an instant. If you are on a diet, you better pass it up.

kathy's herbal butter spread *

1 cup softened butter
⅓ cup parsley, minced
2 large basil leaves, minced
1 large fat clove of garlic, pressed

1. Mix all ingredients well and serve with an especially good bread.

The lecithin included in this recipe may be found in health food stores. This butter/-margarine substitute is healthier than either butter or margarine and always spreads easily, but it must be kept in the refrigerator when not in use. I do not include salt, but you may want to add it. It is also very easy to add herbs, garlic and spices if you want to make a special spread.

butter blend *

2 sticks sweet butter, softened
1 cup safflower oil
2 tbsp. dried milk
¼ tsp. lecithin

1. Place all ingredients in blender and whip.
2. Place in a covered container and keep in the refrigerator.

I like this hot dip because it's unusual and easy to make.

hot artichoke dip *

1 cup artichoke hearts chopped into small pieces
1 cup parmesan cheese
½ cup scallions, chopped
¾ cup mayonnaise
½ tsp. garlic salt
½ tsp. parsley, chopped
½ tsp. pepper
paprika

1. Mix all ingredients except paprika.
2. Spread in a small baking dish.
3. Sprinkle with paprika.
4. Bake at 350 degrees for 20 to 25 minutes.
5. Serve with raw vegetables, crackers, or chips.

black bean dip **

2 cups onions, chopped
⅓ cup peanut oil
2 cups black beans, cooked
1 large clove garlic, pressed with a garlic press
2 tsp. cumin
1 tsp. tabasco sauce
3 tsp. wine vinegar
1½ tsp. salt
½ tsp. pepper
Cooking water from the beans

Note: Beans should be soaked overnight in a large pot of water and cooked until tender the next day.

1. Saute onions in oil until soft.
2. Place onions in bowl and stir in beans.
3. Add garlic puree, cumin, tabasco, vinegar, salt and pepper and stir.
4. Place in blender and add enough of the cooking water, so that you are able to blend the mixture to a good consistency for dipping.
5. Blend well and serve with corn chips.

sally maruscak's clam dip *

1 cup minced clams
1½ cups cottage cheese
½ cup sour cream or yogurt
3 tbsp. minced onions
2 tsp. Worcestershire Sauce
juice of 1 lemon
¼ tsp. salt
½ tsp. pepper
2 tbsp. chives or scallions, minced

1. Mix all ingredients except chives or scallions.
2. Sprinkle chives or scallions on top and serve at room temperature.

Who has ever heard of warm, pickled onions? I never had until they were served to me down in Memphis, Tenn. as an accompaniment to fried catfish.

pickled onions *

4 cups onions, thinly sliced
¾ cups water
¼ cup white vinegar

1. Simmer the onions in water and vinegar for 5 minutes.
2. Serve as a side dish, preferably with fried fish.

To make this dip, you need to save some of the water the beans were cooked in or the liquid from the can, if you used canned beans.

jala-pinto dip **

2 tbsp. oil
1 medium onion, diced
1½ tsp. garlic powder
2½ tsp. chili powder
¾ tsp. cumin
¼ tsp. oregano
½ cup tomato sauce
2 cups cooked jala-pinto beans
½ cup bean juice
2 tsp. jalapeno peppers, minced
¾ tsp. salt
3 tsp. raw onion, minced

1. Heat oil in a skillet and saute onion with garlic powder, chili powder, cumin and oregano for 4 minutes, stirring constantly.
2. Add tomato sauce, beans, bean juice, peppers and salt and simmer over low heat for 15 minutes, stirring occasionally.
3. Place dip in bowl, sprinkle raw onion on top and serve with corn chips, crackers, or raw vegetables.

soups

I finally realized, after all these years, why the soups I used to make were never as good, or as hearty and tasty as I would have liked. It was because I had always believed in that old saw about good soups being made out of a few bones and whatever leftovers were around — a few potatoes, a carrot etc. One night I tasted a delicious soup made by Armand and thought, "Why can't I make something like that?" When he donated the recipe to me, I realized that I had been scrimping too much. It may have been economical, but it didn't taste special. So here is Armand's soup, the soup that changed my style.

armand la macchia's chicken soup **

1 chicken, either whole or cut in pieces
1 tsp. salt
½ tsp. pepper
½ tsp. poultry seasoning
1 medium sized onion, chopped
3 carrots, sliced
½ stalk celery, chopped
½ lb. fresh spinach
1 egg. beaten
4 bouillon cubes
1 lb. macaroni such as shells, corkscrews etc.
½ lb. sweet sausage meat, removed from casings and chopped into small pieces
dash of tabasco sauce
1 cup Romano cheese as a side dish

1. Stew the chicken in a large pot with salt, pepper, and poultry seasoning, and enough water to cover the whole chicken for about 45 minutes or until chicken is done.
2. Remove any foam that has accumulated and set chicken aside.
3. Add all vegetables to broth and cook for 15 minutes.
4. In the meantime, take all the chicken meat from the bones and cut into small pieces. Do not use the skin.
5. Return chicken pieces to pot along with the beaten egg, bouillon cubes, macaroni, sausage and tabasco sauce.
6. Bring to a boil and lower heat; cook for 15 minutes.
7. Check for seasonings.
8. Serve in large, individual soup bowls with cheese on the side.

This soup is easy to make and a good way to use up leftover corn on the cob. Dorothy says she cuts the corn off the cob in the summer when the corn is fresh and the price is low. Then she freezes the kernels in freezer bags to be used throughout the rest of the year.

dorothy's corn chowder *

1 small onion, minced
1 tbsp. butter
4 cups rich chicken broth
1 1/4 cups corn
2 tbsp. dried skim milk
3/4 tbsp. curry powder
salt and fresh ground black pepper

1. Saute onion in butter until soft.
2. Put onions, 1 cup chicken broth, 1 cup of the corn, skim milk, and spices in blender and blend at low speed until smooth.
3. Place in pan with the rest of the broth and heat thoroughly.
4. When ready to serve, garnish with the remaining corn.

I have done a lot of experimenting with this particular recipe because it happens to be one of my favorite soups and I always order it when I eat at a Thai restaurant. It is not terribly difficult, but there are three crucial ingredients which must be purchased in a specialty store. I can't find any American substitutions, so if you can't buy citrus leaves, lemon grass, and galangal roots, you probably should pass this one up. I buy the coconut in a health food store so I can get a pure product. Save the pulp for making the coconut cake in the dessert section, or any other recipe.

thailand coconut soup **

2 cups coconut
2 cups milk
4 cups rich chicken broth
2 dried citrus leaves (by maglood)
2 heaping tsp. dried lemon grass (da kry)
1 piece of dried galangal root(ka) — about the size of a quarter
2 tbsp. fish sauce (found in many Chinese sections)
1 cup cooked chicken, minced
¾ cup mushrooms, sliced in small pieces
juice of one nice sized lime
1½ tbsp. chili powder
½ cups milk
½ cup cream
1 tbsp. fresh coriander, chopped, if available. Otherwise use flat Italian parsley.

1. Bring the coconut and milk to a boil.
2. Let sit for 20 minutes and then press through strainer. You should have ¼ to ½ cup of coconut milk. Reserve.
3. Place chicken broth, citrus leaves, lemon grass, galangal root and fish sauce in a soup pot.
4. Bring to a boil, cover, lower heat and simmer 10 minutes.
5. Add chicken and mushrooms and simmer 4 or 5 minutes.
6. Add lime juice, chili powder, the coconut milk, and cream; bring to a boil, and remove from heat.
7. Sprinkle with coriander or parsley and serve.

An unusual soup and especially tasty in hot summer weather, this comes from Mrs. Acheson, the mother of my good friend, Chris Italiani.

mrs. acheson's cucumber and buttermilk soup *

2 tbsp. oil
2 lbs. cucumber, peeled and cubed
1 cup onion, diced
1 large potato, cooked, peeled and cubed
2 cups chicken broth
2 cups buttermilk
salt and pepper
chives and radish slices for garnish.

1. Saute cucumbers, onions, and potatoes in oil for 5 minutes.
2. Add broth, bring to a boil, cover, lower heat and simmer for 20 minutes.
3. Cool and then blend in blender or food processor.
4. Add buttermilk, salt and pepper and cool for at least two hours in refrigerator.
5. Garnish with chopped chives and radish slices.

tomato-clam soup Oriental style **

1½ dozen little neck clams
4 cups rich chicken broth
2 tbsp. oil
3 tomatoes
3 tbsp. Chinese sesame seed oil
salt and pepper
1½ tbsp. corn starch
3 tbsp. water
½ cup slivered scallion tops

1. Steam clams in a small amount of boiling water until the clams open.
2. Remove clams from shells and set aside.
3. Skin tomatoes by placing in boiling water for a minute or two and then peeling with a sharp knife.
4. Chop tomatoes and saute in oil for five minutes over a low flame.
5. Transfer tomatoes to a soup pot and add clams, chicken broth, sesame seed oil, salt and pepper.
6. Blend corn starch with 3 tbsp. water and add to soup.
7. Simmer gently for 20 minutes.
8. Place in soup tureen or individual soup bowls, garnish with the scallion tops and serve.

My mother-in-law, Marcia, makes a wonderful borscht. She, in turn, says that she got the recipe from her mother, Chaya, and that "they don't make borscht like that anymore." This recipe calls for dried lima beans and if you prefer to use frozen ones, omit the directions for dry lima beans and add the frozen ones at the end with the potatoes. Marcia says that the secret of this borscht is to get the right blend of lemon and sugar. Borscht is a hearty soup that is delicious on a cold night with black bread.

chaya's borscht **

½ cup dried lima beans
2½ qts. water
2 or 3 small veal or beef soup bones
1 small piece of flanken, chuck steak, or beef short ribs — about 2 lbs.
1 large onion, diced
1 8-oz, can tomato sauce
1 lb. head of cabbage, shredded and grated
1 bunch of beets, peeled and grated
juice from 1 lemon, more if necessary
salt and pepper
¼ cup sugar
1 large potato, peeled and cut in quarters
2 cloves garlic, peeled

1. Soak the lima beans overnight in a large pot of water.
2. Drain beans and place in a soup pot with 2½ quarts of water, the soup bones and flanken or other cut of meat.
3. Bring water to a boil, skim off all foam; add remaining ingredients except for potatoes and garlic.
4. Cook over low heat for 2 to 3 hours, or until lima beans are done.
5. Add the potatoes and garlic and cook 20 minutes more.
6. Check to see if you might need more lemon and/or sugar and serve piping hot.

My husband Marty and I were in Zurich, Switzerland for a few days and having a frustrating time finding a nice place to eat. We made a long trip to one restaurant specializing in fondu and found that they were "all out," if you can imagine that in Switzerland! We were staying in a charming place on a hill run by the Ladies Temperance Society, so no wine, of course, in *their* dining room. They had posted a very emphatic announcement that no liquor would be served "even if prescribed by a doctor." Finally someone suggested a place right around the corner and, surprisingly enough, right under our noses, there was an excellent restaurant. Marty had a lovely soup and when I returned home, I tried to duplicate it. It must have a very rich chicken broth as a base.

zurich avocado soup **

- 1 medium onion, minced
- 1 medium green pepper, seeded and minced
- 1 medium red pepper, seeded and minced
- 1½ cup mushrooms, sliced
- 3 tbsp. butter
- 6 cups rich chicken broth
- 1 large avacado, ripe but firm, peeled and cut in small chunks
- kernels from two large ears of corn, or ½ to 1 cup frozen corn
- ½ tsp. salt
- ¼ tsp. black pepper
- ¼ tsp. cayenne pepper
- 2 fresh basil leaves, minced
- 2 tbsp. flour
- 4 tbsp. water
- juice from 1 lemon
- ½ cup heavy cream

1. Saute onions, peppers and mushrooms in butter until soft.
2. Transfer onions, peppers, and mushrooms to a large soup pot and add chicken stock, avocado, corn and all the spices; cook over low heat for ½ hour.
3. Mix flour and water together, add to soup and cook 10 minutes.
4. Stir in lemon juice and heavy cream and cook for 10 more minutes.
5. Serve very hot with crusty French bread.

salads and dressings

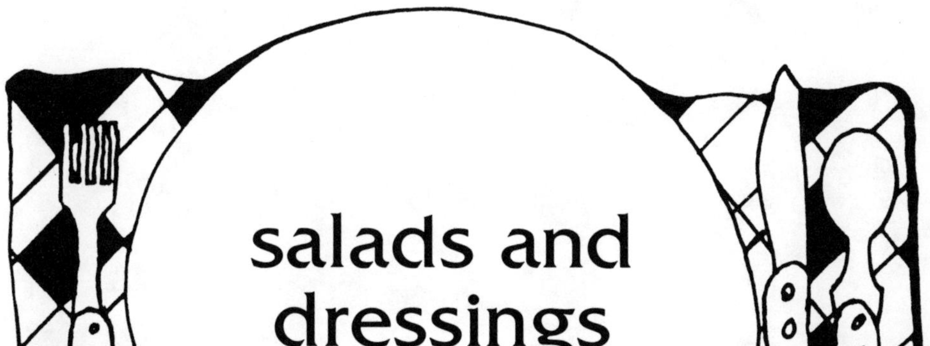

An excellent and healthy recipe for tofu, this comes from a lady named Rhoda whom I have never met. She did some pasteup work for my first cookbook and sent me this to include in my second one. For those people who love egg salad, but don't want to include too many eggs in their diet, tofu salad is an awfully good substitute. It can also be used as a sandwich spread on a good bread.

rhoda's tofu salad *

12 oz. tofu
1 stalk celery, chopped
¼ cup minced onion
1 tbsp. minced parsley
¼ tsp turmeric
½ tsp. dill leaves
½ tsp. salt
¼ tsp. dry mustard
¼ tsp. celery salt
¼ tsp. pepper
salad greens
1½ cups alfalfa sprouts
1½ tbsp. mayonnaise

1. Combine all ingredients in blender except sprouts and greens and mix well.
2. Serve on greens and sprinkle sprouts on top.

At one of our communal meals, a young man spoke with great enthusiasm about how he loved to create dishes and asked if he could send me some of his creations for my cookbook. It was with a certain surprise that I discovered that the dish that intrigued me the most at this dinner was his carrot salad.

john's carrot creation **

3 cups raw carrots, shredded
½ cup feta cheese, broken up in small bits
½ cup olives without the pimentoes
2 scallions, cut in 1-inch slivers
⅓ cup pignoli nuts
¼ cup olive oil
juice of one large lemon
¼ tsp. garlic salt
¼ tsp. white pepper

1. Mix carrots, cheese, olives, scallions, and nuts with the olive oil until well coated.
2. Add lemon juice, garlic salt and pepper; stir.

Judy Wolfe, or just plain Wolfe as she likes to be called, has also collected her friends' recipes and lent me her collection when I was doing this one. These are two nice side dishes that she got from her friend Carlos Lindgrin, so you can see how recipes get passed around out here. I don't know Carlos, but Judy is a very special friend. Not only is she invaluable in helping my husband and me in our publishing business, but she is great fun to have around. She has a unique way of expressing herself and always seems to say the unexpected. She has often done the unexpected too. When she was younger, she decided that she would have a child at 20 and then one at 40. After raising son Daniel, she gave birth to Conor 21 years later, only one year off schedule.

carlos' spicy chinese cukes *

2 cucumbers, peeled and sliced very thin
4 tbsp. light sesame oil
4 tbsp. tamari
2 tbsp. sugar
½ tbsp. salt
½ tbsp. tabasco
2 tbsp. rice vinegar

1. Mix cucumbers with the sesame oil until well coated.
2. Mix the tamari, sugar, salt and tabasco in a small bowl and add to the cucumbers.
3. Last, add the vinegar, mix, and chill before serving.

carlos' bean sprout salad *

3 cups fresh bean sprouts
¼ cup scallions, chopped
¼ cup pimento, cut in thin strips
1 garlic clove, minced
¼ cup peanut oil
½ tbsp. salt
1 tbsp. pepper
2 tbsp. tamari
2 tbsp. rice vinegar
2 tbsp. ground, toasted sesame seeds

1. Mix sprouts, scallions, pimento, and garlic.
2. Add oil, salt and pepper and mix well.
3. Add tamari and vinegar and mix again.
4. Sprinkle ground sesame seeds on top and chill for 20 minutes before serving.

This is best prepared one day in advance. Yogurt can be substituted for the sour cream.

mrs. acheson's beet and apple salad *

- ¾ tsp. dry mustard
- 1 tbsp. sugar
- ½ tsp. Worcestershire Sauce
- 2 tbsp. wine vinegar
- ¼ tsp. salt
- ¼ tsp. pepper
- ¾ cup sour cream
- 1 16 oz. jar of pickled beets, drained
- 2 medium apples, peeled and cubed
- 1 medium cucumber, peeled and cubed

1. Mix mustard, sugar, Worcestershire sauce, vinegar, salt, pepper and sour cream.
2. In another bowl, mix the drained beets with apples and cucumber.
3. Add dressing to the beet mixture and stir well.
4. Chill overnight before serving.

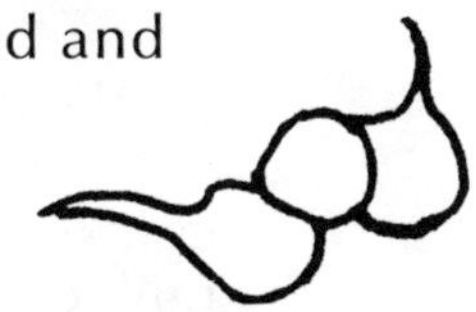

During a visit to Baltimore we were given an unexpected dinner invitation. The fine meal was cooked by a psychiatrist named Rita Lautz. She graciously donated this salad recipe. It should be served as soon as you add the hot dressing.

rita lautz's hot salad **

- 8 slices lean bacon
- 1 small onion, minced
- 2 eggs beaten
- 2 tbsp. cornstarch
- ½ cup cider vinegar
- ½ cup sugar
- 1 tsp. salt
- 1 tsp. pepper
- 1 head of lettuce or other salad greens, washed, dried, and torn into pieces

1. Fry bacon and onions over low heat until bacon is done.
2. Drain bacon and onions, cool and cut bacon into small pieces. Reserve.
3. Add cornstarch to beaten eggs and stir well.
4. Put into small saucepan and add vinegar, sugar, salt and pepper.
5. Stir over medium heat until thickened.
6. Put greens into a serving bowl and toss with dressing.
7. Add bacon and onion and toss lightly.
8. Serve immediately.

We have a friend named Michael Barrett who doesn't cook at all. He bought a very good restaurant in the city so he could eat nicely. One day, out at his country house, he said, "I'm going to have lunch at my friend Alan's house. Why don't you all come with me?" He then called Alan and said, "I'm bringing some friends for lunch. Put more apples in the chicken salad." Alan is a most gracious host. Michael brought at least eight of us. We spent all day in his beautiful pool and ate a lovely chicken salad with apples cooked by a young man who was just learning to be a chef. You can leave out the vodka as I usually do. It's just as good.

a special chicken salad ***

2 chicken breasts, skinned, boned, and cut into bite sized pieces
1 tbsp. vodka
5 tbsp. orange juice
2 tbsp. olive oil
2 tbsp. dry vermouth
½ cup diced celery
¼ cup diced onions
½ cup diced cucumber
2 apples, skinned and diced
½ cup mayonnaise
¼ cup yogurt
3 tbsp. Dijon mustard
salt and pepper
½ cup parsley, minced

1. Marinate chicken pieces in vodka and orange juice overnight, or at least 4 hours.
2. Drain chicken and saute in olive oil over medium heat until done (when chicken has turned white and lost its pink color).
3. Put chicken in a bowl with vermouth, celery, onion, cucumber, and apples.
4. Make a sauce of mayonnaise, yogurt, mustard, salt and pepper.
5. Mix with the chicken and garnish with parsley.

A couple of years ago, I was in New York City studying acting with Uta Hagen, a fine actress, an excellent teacher and a wonderful cook, who, incidentally, has written a very fine cookbook of her own. In each of her classes two people would donate food for all to share during the break. I thought that this donation was a nice variation of a common dish.

curried tuna salad *

- 2 6½ cans tunafish, drained
- 1 small onion, minced
- ¾ cup mayonnaise
- 1 tbsp. curry powder
- 1 cup cooked peas, either canned or frozen, but well drained.
- salad greens

1. Chop tunafish well and add minced onions.
2. Mix mayonnaise with the curry powder and add to tunafish. Mix well.
3. Gently add peas to mixture and serve on bed of salad greens.

Chris Italiani is a good friend who teaches languages at the high school out here. She is warm, independent and has a good sense of humor. Widowed when her son was only two years old, she has had to learn to pinch pennies at various times in her life and this recipe is a good example of how she did it. I don't like any of the potato salads made in delicatessens, but I love this one that Chris makes.

chris' potato salad **

- 6 cups peeled, cubed potatoes
- ½ cup finely diced carrots
- ½ cup finely diced celery
- 1 cup minced onion
- ½ cup sliced olives
- ¼ cup safflower oil
- 2 tsp. dry mustard
- 3 tbsp. dried dill (or 1 cup fresh dill)
- ⅓ cup minced parsley
- salt and pepper
- 5 tbsp. vinegar

1. Put potatoes, carrots, celery, onions, and olives in a large salad bowl.
2. Make a dressing of the oil, mustard, dill, parsley, salt, and pepper; gently toss the potato salad to coat well.
3. Add the vinegar and toss briefly again.

My husband was determined to grow his own potatoes out here on Long Island. What we harvested were lots of tiny and odd shaped potatoes, too small or strange to peel. I remembered having some kind of hot potato salad with bacon out in Indiana many years ago. Hence this dish. I used unskinned new potatoes, but most people like them skinned.

hot potato salad **

2 lbs. potatoes
5 slices of bacon
2 tbsp. bacon drippings
1½ tbsp. raw sugar
1½ tsp. flour
salt and pepper
⅓ cup cider vinegar
⅔ cup water
1 large onion, chopped
2 tbsp. chopped dill
2 tbsp. chopped parsley

1. Boil potatoes until done; drain and slice.
2. Fry bacon until crisp, drain well and crumble.
3. Remove all but about 2 tbsp. of bacon drippings from pan.
4. Add sugar, flour, salt, pepper, vinegar, and water and cook slightly over low heat stirring to make a smooth sauce.
5. Add onion and cook 3 minutes.
6. Add potatoes and bacon and cook to heat through.
7. Place in serving bowl and sprinkle with dill and parsley.

I sometimes see pictures of dishes that look so pretty that I cut them out to try and duplicate them at a later time. This was such a salad and all I have is the picture. The different ingredients are not mixed together, but put on the plate separately and arranged in a pretty pattern. Then I pour the dressing over it. I like a simple dressing best, made with lemon juice and olive oil.

super salad *

1 head Boston lettuce, separated into leaves
2 Belgian endives, separated into leaves
1 cup radishes, sliced
1 large avocado, skinned and cubed
2 cups orange sections

1. Arrange all ingredients on a platter.
2. Pour dressing over it and serve immediately.

Dressing

4 tbsp. olive oil
juice from 1 to 2 lemons
salt and pepper

1. Put in small jar and shake well before pouring over salad.

Too often, the zucchini in my refrigerator ends up being thrown away because it has started to spoil. One of the reasons I have it in the first place is because it seems to grow abundantly in so many of our friend's gardens and they don't know what to do with it either. The following recipe is my own invention and came out of my determination not to let another zucchini get relagated to the garbage can.

marinated zucchini salad **

3 tbsp. safflower oil
3 zucchini, sliced
2 stalks celery, sliced
3 tbsp. water
2 cloves garlic, minced
1 medium onion, diced
2 tomatoes, diced
1½ cups any kind of cooked beans (green beans, kidney beans, fava beans or chickpeas). Freshly cooked beans are best. Frozen or canned will do.
3 tbsp. fresh parsley
½ tsp. basil
½ tsp. chervil
6 tbsp. olive oil
6 tbsp. wine vinegar
salt and pepper

1. Saute zucchini and celery in safflower oil for a few moments.
2. Add 3 tbsp. water, cover, turn heat low and cook until the zucchini is done. Do not overcook; it should be crunchy.
3. Drain zucchini and celery and place in a salad bowl with garlic, onions, and tomatoes.
4. Drain beans well and add to bowl along with parsley, basil and chervil.
5. Add olive oil and toss salad thoroughly.
6. Add vinegar, salt and pepper and mix well.
7. Refrigerate for at least 3 hours before serving.

Along with the soup that we had in Zurich, Switzerland, which is included in the last chapter, we also had a lovely salad. This can be used as a main dish for a summer meal or as a very fancy accompaniment to dinner.

zurich shrimp and avocado salad ***

greens for 4 people
1 cup alfalfa sprouts
1 large avocado, sliced
2 tomatoes, sliced
1 large tart apple, peeled and sliced
½ lb. cooked shrimp, cleaned
1 cup mayonnaise
¼ cup catsup
¼ cup milk
3 tbsp. horseradish
salt and pepper
2 scallions, chopped fine

1. Arrange greens and sprouts in individual salad bowls.
2. Divide avocado, tomatoes, apple and shrimp and put some in each bowl.
3. When ready to serve, mix mayonnaise, catsup, milk, horseradish, salt and pepper and put some on top of each salad.
4. Garnish with scallions.

chicken salad a la balducci **

4 chicken breasts
1 small onion, sliced
1 stalk celery, sliced
1 cup cooked artichoke hearts, sliced
6 cherry tomatoes
¾ cup sour cream
½ cup mayonnaise
½ cup yogurt
4 tbsp. tarragon
salt and pepper

1. Simmer chicken breasts, onion, carrots and celery in 2 quarts water until chicken is done.
2. Reserve broth for soup and prepare chicken by de-boning and removing skin.
3. Cut chicken into bite-sized chunks.
4. Mix chicken, artichoke hearts, and tomatoes.
5. Mix sour cream, mayonnaise, yogurt, tarragon, salt and pepper in a separate bowl.
6. Place chicken in a serving bowl and pour the dressing over it, stirring well.
6. Chill before serving.

greek marinated vegetables **

1 small head of cauliflower, trimmed and broken into flowerets
½ pound mushrooms, wiped off and sliced
1 8½ oz. can artichokes, drained and cut in half
⅓ cup olive oil
1 large clove garlic, minced
½ tsp. oregano
½ tsp. basil
salt and pepper
⅓ cup wine vinegar

1. Steam cauliflower until done. It should be crunchy, not mushy. Drain.
2. Place in salad bowl with mushrooms and artichokes.
3. Add olive oil, garlic, herbs, salt and pepper; toss well.
4. Add vinegar; toss again and serve chilled.

I usually like some kind of salad with dinner, but an ordinary salad doesn't seem to fit in if the meal is Chinese. I had this one time at someone's house and rushed home to add it to my collection.

chinese cabbage salad *

1 small cabbage, shredded
1 onion, sliced thin
4 tbsp. sesame oil
3 tbsp. rice wine vinegar
salt

1. Parboil the cabbage and onions in boiling water until they are softened but still crunchy. Drain.
2. Mix the cabbage and onions with the sesame oil to coat well.
3. Add the vinegar and salt and let sit a couple of hours before serving.

This is another simple salad to accompany Chinese dishes which I concocted because I like something cold and crisp with Chinese food. You could substitute almost anything as long as you use rice wine vinegar and sesame oil.

chinese salad *

1 cucumber, peeled and sliced very thin
1 tomato, sliced thin
1 green pepper, seeded and cut into thin strips
1 onion, sliced and separated into rings
¼ tsp. celery salt
salt and pepper
3 tbsp. dark sesame oil
3 tbsp. rice wine vinegar
4 tbsp. sesame seeds

1. Mix all vegetables in a salad bowl.
2. Add celery salt, salt, pepper and oil; toss well.
3. Add vinegar and mix.
4. Sprinkle with sesame seeds.

A pretty and vivacious woman named Belle contributed a rather difficult but very good oriental noodle dish elsewhere in this book. However, she also gave me this simple salad dressing to balance it out. I make enough to have on hand for a couple of days.

belle's mustard dressing *

¾ cup olive oil
1¼ tsp. dry mustard
1 tsp. sugar
½ tsp. salt
½ tsp. pepper
1 tsp. Worcestershire sauce
¼ cup good wine vinegar

1. Place all ingredients in a covered jar and shake well before using it on salad.

sour cream/roquefort dressing *

1¼ oz. Roquefort cheese
1 tbsp. oil
½ cup sour cream
2 tbsp. lemon juice
salt and pepper

1. Crumble cheese and mix well with oil.
2. Add the rest of the ingredients and stir.

sour cream dressing *

½ cup sour cream or yogurt
3 tbsp. wine vinegar
½ tsp. sugar
¼ tsp. salt
¼ tsp. paprika
½ tsp. dry mustard
1½ tsp. tomato paste or puree
freshly ground black pepper

1. Mix all ingredients and pour on salad; then add freshly ground black pepper.

tomato dressing *

⅔ cup safflower oil
⅓ cup red wine vinegar
¼ cup tomato juice
1 tsp. grated onion
1 tsp. grated green pepper
¼ tsp. dry mustard
½ tsp. Worcestershire sauce
dash of tabasco sauce
1 clove garlic
salt and pepper

1. Mix all ingredients in a jar and store in refrigerator.
2. Shake well before using on salads.

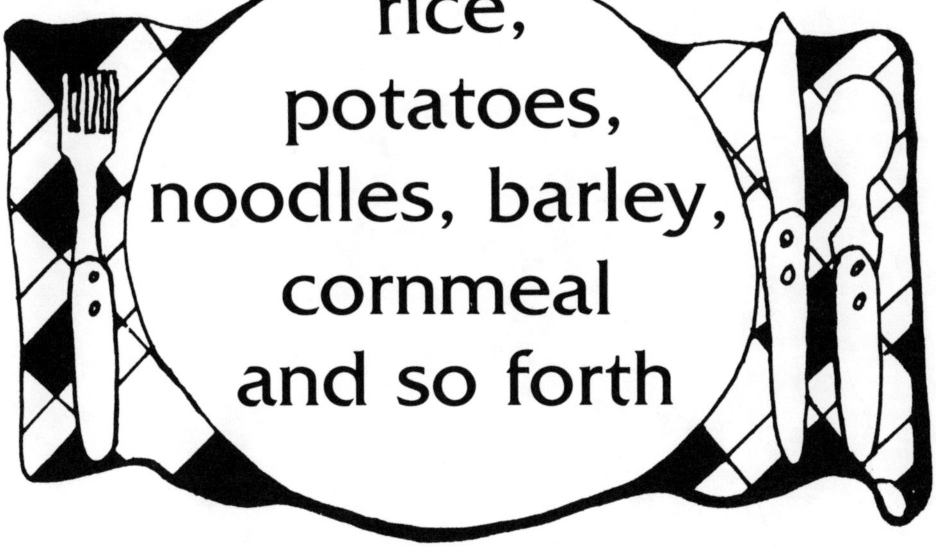
rice,
potatoes,
noodles, barley,
cornmeal
and so forth

Jeanne Humphries had a couple of nice recipes in my last cookbook and willingly donated another to this one. The pilaf can be the basis for a whole meal and it's particularly good with a roast pork loin, I found.

jeanne's pilaf *

5 tbsp. butter
1 large clove garlic, minced
2 medium onions, chopped
1½ stalks celery, sliced diagonally
1 small green pepper, seeded and chopped
1 cup brown rice
2⅔ cup boiling water
2 bouillon cubes
½ tsp. salt
¼ tsp. black pepper
dash of cayenne pepper
1 generous cup raisins

1. Saute garlic, onions, celery and green pepper in butter until onions are transparent.
2. Add rice and saute 5 minutes more over low heat, stirring frequently.
3. Add boiling water, bouillon cubes, salt, black pepper, cayenne pepper and raisins.
4. Stir over high heat until the mixture comes to a boil, then reduce heat, cover, and simmer until rice is done (50 to 60 minutes).

Priscilla Bollard was my speech teacher many years ago when I attended The Neighborhood Playhouse School of the Theatre in New York. I have always remained friends with her because she is a very special person, warm and caring. When her husband died tragically, she raised her three young children and went back to college receiving a doctorate in speech pathology. She served me this rice stuffing years ago and it's a nice change from the usual bread and giblets. It should be enough to stuff a 4 to 6 lb. chicken.

priscilla's rice and apricot stuffing *

2 cups cold rice
3 tbsp. melted butter
3 tbsp. chopped parsley
3 tbsp. chives
½ cup finely chopped celery tops
⅛ tsp. thyme
⅛ tsp. cloves
⅛ tsp. mace
salt and pepper
1 cup finely chopped dried apricots

1. Mix all ingredients together.
2. Chill in refrigerator for one hour before stuffing.

My friend, Don Mathews, from Argentina had a recipe for a delicious stew in my first cookbook. However, he said that what I listed as Argentine Potato Pie in that book was really a "tortilla" and he would send me the recipe for the authentic Argentine Potato Pie. He also remarked that it was a good dish to make ahead of time and it could be stored nicely in the freezer. He wished us all "Buen provecho."

don mathew's argentine potato pie **

1 tbsp. oil
1 clove garlic, chopped
1 medium onion, chopped
2 lbs. ground lean beef
salt and pepper to taste
1/8 tsp. red pepper
1 bay leaf
12 green olives, chopped
1 tbsp. seedless raisins
2 hardboiled eggs, sliced
2 lbs. mashed potatoes seasoned with salt, pepper, and a little nutmeg
1 egg yolk, beaten

1. Heat oil in skillet and saute garlic and onion until transparent.
2. Add ground meat, salt, pepper, red pepper, and bay leaf and stir fry until meat has lost its pink color.
3. Remove from heat and add olives and raisins.
4. Pour into a large deep casserole and arrange the sliced eggs over the meat.
5. Cover with mashed potatoes.
6. Smooth the surface and then scratch with a fork to decorate.
7. Baste with the egg yolk and place in a 350 degree oven until warm — about 20 minutes. If you have frozen it, of course, it will take longer to heat.

I always have leftover rice somehow, so was happy to be given this dish by my friend, Ginger. It can be made ahead of time and used for any meal, including breakfast for a change.

rice pancakes *

1 cup cooked rice, white or brown
1 tbsp. melted butter
1 cup skim milk
1 tsp. salt
1 tsp. sugar
1 egg, beaten
1 cup flour, sifted
2 tsp. baking powder, sifted
4 tbsp. safflower oil

1. Mix all ingredients together.
2. Heat oil in heavy frying pan.
3. When oil sizzles, drop by large spoonfuls in pan and fry until nicely browned.
4. Flip onto other side and brown.
5. Serve plain with salt and pepper, or with sour cream or yogurt.

When my friend, Craig Braun came out to visit last summer he brought the delightful Belle (whose mustard dressing appeared earlier) with him. She proceeded to make us a delicious and exotic dish. Later on, she sent me the recipe; meticulously written on three pages of paper with all kinds of advice and hints. Her dish was very, very hot and I have modified it somewhat. You may even want to make it milder. There are many things you can add, says Belle, but to simplify it, I am just giving the standard version. It is not as difficult as it may seem, especially if you assemble everything first. If it becomes a little too dry, add more sesame oil.

belle's chinese noodles ***

- ¼ cup hoisin sauce (found in the Chinese section of most supermarkets)
- 1 tbsp. sesame oil
- 1 tsp. soy sauce
- 1 tsp. Chinese chili sauce with garlic
- ¼ cup raw sugar
- ¾ tsp. cayenne pepper
- 1 chicken breast, cooked and cut in small pieces
- ½ lb. bean curd, cut in small pieces
- 10 oz. thin noodles, preferably whole wheat
- ⅛ cup sesame oil
- 2 eggs, beaten
- 1 bunch of scallions, chopped in 2 in. pieces.
- 1 cup peanuts, ground
- ¼ cup sesame seeds

1. Mix hoisin sauce, sesame oil, soy sauce and Chinese chili sauce together.
2. Mix sugar with the cayenne pepper.
3. Cook and chop chicken into small pieces; cut bean curd into small pieces.
4. Heat a large pot of water to boiling and drop noodles into water.
5. Cook until *al dente* and drain well.
6. Heat the ⅛ cup sesame oil in wok and then add noodles.
7. Stir fry for a moment just to coat them.
8. Make a hole in the center of noodles, pour in eggs and scramble briefly.
9. Add hoisin sauce mixture and stir well.
10. Add raw sugar and cayenne and stir again.
11. Add chicken, bean curd, scallions, and peanuts and stir fry until everything is well mixed.
12. Sprinkle with sesame seeds and serve hot or cold.

Sesame Noodles is an unusual and interesting dish given to me by Judy Wolfe. It has taken me a number of times to get the measurements correct since Judy just lists ingredients. You may want to doctor them a little to suit your taste. When I finally made it successfully for one of our music sessions, four of my friends asked for the recipe. I am not sure of the geographic origins of this dish, but it is unique, can be served hot or cold and is a little easier to prepare than Belle's Chinese Noodles. You can add diced, cooked white chicken if you wish.

sesame noodles **

1 lb. thin linguine or whole wheat noodles
2 tbsp. dark sesame seed oil with chilis
½ cup sesame seed paste (tahini)
1 cup chunky peanut butter
2 tbsp. rice wine vinegar
2 tbsp. raw sugar
2 tbsp. soy sauce (tamari)
water
2 tbsp. dark sesame seed oil
2 tbsp. peanut oil
⅓ cup minced scallions

1. Cook noodles in large pot of boiling water.
2. While noodles are cooking, make a smooth sauce of dark sesame seed oil with chilis, sesame seed paste, peanut butter, vinegar, sugar, soy sauce and enough water to give it a smooth consistency.
3. Drain noodles and coat well with the remaining dark sesame seed oil and the peanut oil.
4. Toss the noodles with the sauce. You may have to add a little more water in order to toss it well.
5. Sprinkle with scallions.

If you want to make your own granola and avoid all the sugar in the supermarket brands, here's one way to do it.

homemade granola **

4 cups oats
1 cup sesame seeds
1 cup cornmeal
1½ cups whole wheat flour
1 cup wheat germ
½ to 1 cup chopped, unsalted nuts
½ cup honey
½ cup safflower oil
1 cup cold water

1. Mix all dry ingredients.
2. Mix honey, oil and water and stir thoroughly into dry ingredients.
3. Spread on bottom of roasting pan or cookie sheet and place in a 250 degree oven.
4. Heat for 1½ hours and stir every 15 minutes or so in order to prevent burning.
5. Place in a covered jar to store.

This is Marty's version of nachos. We had it in a splendid Mexican restaurant up near Lake Placid, N.Y.

marty's cheese nachos **

10 corn tortillas (usually available in supermarkets)
corn oil
1½ Montery Jack cheese, grated
⅔ to 1 cup hot jalapeno peppers, sliced. (The amount depends on how hot you like your food.)

1. Stack tortillas on top of each other and cut in sixths.
2. Add enough corn oil to cover the bottom of a large frying pan. You might have to cook these in shifts; you should have enough oil so that it bubbles around the tortillas.
3. Fry over medium heat until the tortillas get a little stiff, turning once. This should take only a few minutes.
4. Drain on paper towels and then spread in a large, flat baking pan. The whole bottom of the pan should be covered, but the tortillas should not overlap, so you may have to use 2 pans.
5. Preheat oven to 375 degrees.
6. Sprinkle cheese over tortillas and then add the peppers. You should try to see that each tortilla has at least one slice of pepper.
7. Cook in oven for about 10 minutes or until cheese is melted and bubbly.
8. Serve immediately. It's very nice with ice cold beer in frosted glasses with a slice of lemon or lime.

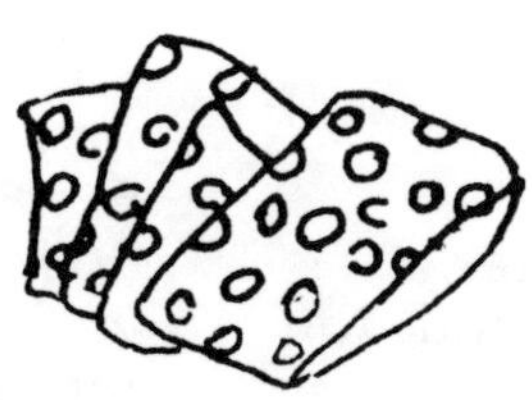

polenta with gorgonzola **

¼ tsp. salt
2 cups cornmeal, yellow or white
3 tbsp. butter
¼ lb. gorgonzola cheese
¼ cup parmesan cheese

1. Bring 2 quarts water to a boil and add salt.
2. Gradually stir in cornmeal with a wire whisk.
3. Lower heat and cook for 40 minutes, stirring often with a wooden spoon. It *will* stick to the sides and bottom of the pan.
4. Very lightly grease a square Pyrex dish and pour the cornmeal into it.
5. Cool for a couple of hours or overnight.
6. When ready to cook, melt butter in a saucepan.
7. Crumble gorgonzola cheese over top of cornmeal.
8. Then drizzle butter and parmesan cheese over it and bake in a 350 degree oven for about 20 minutes or until heated thoroughly.
9. Cool slightly, cut into squares and serve.

This is another way to use up cooked rice which my family likes. I use hot chilis. If you don't like spicy foods, use green chilis.

hot chili rice *

2 large hot chilis or 1 4-oz. can green chilis
1½ cups yogurt
1½ cups sour cream
3 cups cooked rice
¾ pound Montery Jack cheese.

1. Chop chilis into small pieces.
2. Mix chilis with yogurt and sour cream.
3. Place half of the rice in a buttered casserole and pour half of the sauce over it.
4. Cut half of the cheese into strips and place over casserole mixture.
5. Add the rest of the rice, the rest of the sauce and cut the remaining cheese into strips and place on top.
6. Bake at 350 degrees, covered for 30 minutes.
7. Remove cover and bake 10 minutes more.

I love french fries, but I don't want to eat them; there's too much fat from deep frying and too much salt. Here's a terrific substitute.

baked potato crisps *

6 nice sized potatoes
garlic salt
paprika
pepper

1. Peel potatoes and cut into thin round slices.
2. Sprinkle with garlic salt, paprika and pepper.
3. Place slices in a large, oiled, flat baking dish, taking care that they don't overlap.
4. Bake in a 400 degree oven for 30 to 40 minutes until nicely browned.

My grandmother used to make this hearty dish and only recently I found that its proper name is "Bubble and Squeak." It comes from England and is properly made with bacon drippings, but I prefer to use safflower oil.

my grandmother's bubble & squeak **

⅓ cup safflower oil
4 cups cabbage, shredded and cooked
2 cups potatoes, cooked, skinned, but not mashed
salt and pepper

1. Mix cabbage well with the cooked potato. The potatoes should be slightly mushy to mix well with the cabbage.
2. Add salt and plenty of pepper.
3. Heat oil in a large, heavy frying pan and then add the mixture.
5. Press it down to make a flat cake and let the bottom get nicely browned. Do not turn.
6. Serve it piping hot and cut in wedges.

How's this for an unusual way to use oatmeal?

oatcakes *

1 onion, minced
1 clove garlic, minced
1 small green pepper, minced
1 green chili, chopped fine
1½ cups oatmeal
1⅓ cups yogurt
¼ tsp. salt
¼ cup safflower oil (more if needed)

1. Mix all ingredients except oil.
2. Heat the oil in a large frying pan and drop the oatcake mixture onto pan as you would pancakes.
3. Fry until brown; then brown on the other side.

I haven't cooked many dishes made with barley. A friend of mine named Rose knew that my husband loves it, so she donated this to my cookbook and whenever I make it, Marty never fails to remark on how good it is.

marty's favorite barley dish **

3½ cups chicken broth
3 cups beef broth
1 cup barley
½ cup onion, chopped
2 stalks celery, chopped
3 tbsp. safflower oil
½ cup white wine
½ cup parmesan cheese
½ cup mushrooms, sliced
salt and pepper

1. Bring 3 cups of the chicken broth and all of the beef broth to a boil and add barley.
2. Turn heat down to low; cover and simmer 1 hour.
3. Saute onions and celery in oil for a few moments.
4. Add wine and continue cooking until the wine is reduced to about half.
5. Add onion mixture to barley along with the extra half cup of chicken broth and simmer 10 minutes.
6. Stir in parmesan cheese, mushrooms, salt and lots of freshly ground black pepper.
7. Cook about 4 minutes more.

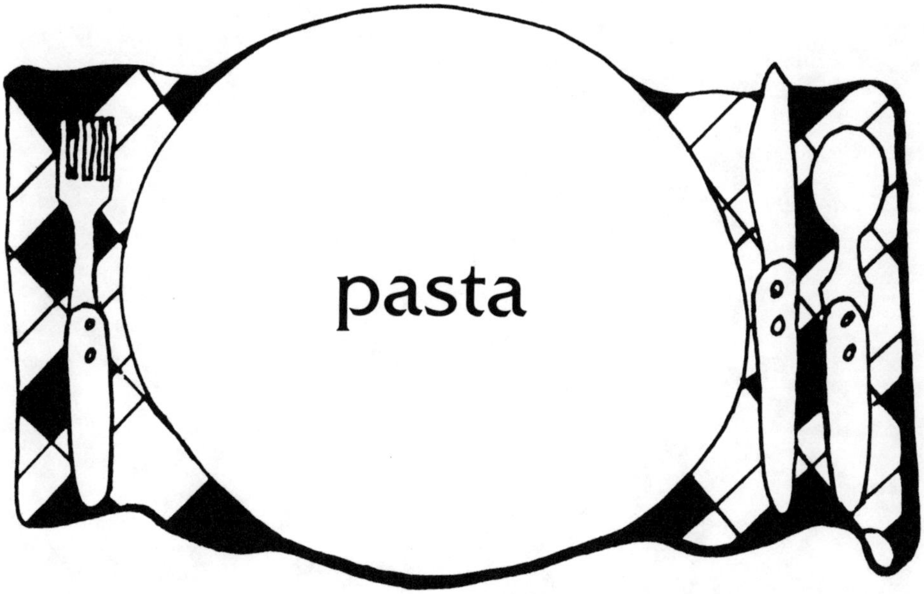

pasta

bernice hunt's pasta alla carbonara **

1 pound spaghetti or fettuchine
4 slices bacon
2 eggs
1 cup heavy cream (more, if needed; see note)
½ cup freshly grated parmesan cheese
½ stick butter
salt and pepper

1. Boil the pasta in salted water according to package directions; do not overcook.
2. Fry the bacon until crisp; drain on paper towels and cut or crumble into small pieces.
3. Beat the eggs in a bowl until frothy; then beat in the cream and cheese.
4. Melt the butter in a very large skillet and add the egg mixture. Cook, stirring, until eggs are barely beginning to set.
5. Add the hot, drained pasta at once and stir in the bacon.
6. Season to taste and serve with additional cheese at the table.

Note: If pasta seems too dry you can add a little more cream.

Carol Lindemann called one late afternoon and said, "Let's make a dinner together. I have a friend who can make pasta and I'll bring artichokes." Carol is a psychologist who specializes in phobias. She lives in New York. but comes out to her country place on weekends. She's nice to spend time with, so I said sure. Over she came with bags of groceries and a young man who proceeded to make a lovely pasta in a matter of minutes. This is it.

a young man's pasta *

1 lb. spaghetti, cooked
5 cloves garlic, minced
5 tbsp. olive oil
1 2-lb. can Italian plum tomatoes
½ cup pitted black olives, sliced
salt and pepper to taste
1 cup grated parmesan cheese

1. Cook pasta and drain
2. Saute the garlic in olive oil until golden, not brown.
3. Drain the tomatoes well and add them to the pan.
4. Mash and stir the tomatoes with a wooden spoon for a few minutes.
5. Add the black olives, salt, and pepper and cook gently for 20 minutes.
6. Add the parmesan cheese to sauce; mix well and serve over pasta.

Marty experimented with this pasta after being smitten with something like it prepared by my sister-in-law, Linda. The cream and butter make it delicious, but rich, so one shouldn't have it once a week. Save it for special occasions.

marty and linda's pasta **

¾ lb. good sweet sausage
1 pint of cream
½ cup grated parmesan cheese
½ stick butter, melted
1 tbsp. cracked pepper
¾ cup minced parsley
1 lb. spaghetti
1 egg, beaten

1. Take the casings off the sausage and brown in a heavy skillet, using a spatula to crumble and making sure the sausage is completely done. It should probably take about 15 minutes.
2. Pour off any excess grease and add the cream, parmesan cheese, butter, cracked pepper and parsley. Cook over low heat for 10 minutes.
3. In the meantime, cook the pasta in a large pot of boiling water.
4. When pasta is *al dente*, drain well and pour into a large serving bowl; immediately add the beaten egg and mix well.
5. Pour the sauce over the pasta and mix again.
6. Serve right away with a bowl of extra cheese on the side.

Chris Thompson is a longtime friend of ours who is many things. She's pretty, bright, and a talented artist as well. She's married to Richard Pannebianco, one of the most handsome and nicest doctors I know. To top it off, they are the proud parents of extraordinary six-year-old twins, Jace and Nova. Richard loves to go scalloping when the season opens and Chris cooked this pasta dish for us one night. It too is extraordinary.

chris's pasta with scallops **

2 tbsp. chopped garlic
3 tbsp. minced parsley
½ cup olive oil
½ lb. scallops, rinsed and patted dry
½ tsp. red pepper flakes
salt and pepper
¼ tsp. basil
1 lb. pasta
½ cup Italian breadcrumbs, toasted
½ cup grated parmesan cheese

1. Saute garlic and parsley in olive oil until garlic is golden.
2. Add scallops, red pepper, salt, pepper, and basil and cook over low heat until scallops turn white.
3. Meanwhile, cook pasta, drain and put in large serving bowl.
4. Add scallop mixture and toss well.
5. Add breadcrumbs and parmesan cheese; mix again.
6. Serve immediately with more parmesan cheese on the side.

An absolutely succulent seafood pasta, this is easy to make and not too expensive, considering the shrimp and clams in it.

seafood pasta **

1 dozen littleneck clams (they seem to be the most tender)
½ cup butter
½ cup olive oil
6 large garlic cloves, minced
1 tsp. oregano
1 tsp. rosemary
1 cup dry white wine
½ lb. shrimp, peeled, de-veined and cut in pieces
1 cup tomatoes, peeled and chopped
½ cup minced flat parsley
salt and pepper
1 cup grated parmesan cheese
1 lb. thin spaghetti

1. Cook clams in a covered pot with a small amount of boiling water until the shells have opened. Reserve clams and discard shells.
2. Melt butter and olive oil in a frying pan over medium heat until bubbly.
3. Add garlic and cook until golden.
4. Add oregano, rosemary and wine and cook until wine has cooked down.
5. Reduce heat and add clams, shrimp, tomatoes, parsley, salt and pepper and cook over low heat for 25 minutes or until the tomatoes have cooked down and the sauce is thick, not watery.
6. In the meantime, cook pasta until done and drain.
7. Mix pasta, sauce and parmesan cheese together and serve.

This is a delicious and unusual dish that I had at Bernice Hunt's house in Bedford, N.Y. When I came back to the Hamptons, I tried to figure out how she had made it. Since she called it Greek Pasta, I decided it must have a little oregano and lemon juice. You want to make sure that your sauce is ample, so it might be necessary to add a little tomato puree, juice, or paste if it has cooked down too much.

greek pasta **

- 3 cloves garlic, minced
- 3 tbsp. olive oil
- 6 nice ripe tomatoes, skinned and chopped (or 1 16-oz. can of tomatoes, drained).
- ½ tsp. sugar
- 1 tbsp. lemon juice
- 1 tsp. oregano
- salt and pepper
- ¾ to 1 lb. shrimp, peeled and deveined (either whole or cut in pieces).
- 1 lb. rigatoni
- ¾ lb. feta cheese

1. Saute garlic in olive oil until lightly browned.
2. Add tomatoes, sugar, lemon juice, oregano, salt and pepper and simmer for 45 minutes.
3. Add shrimp and cook 10 minutes more or until it has lost its pink color.
4. In the meantime, cook the rigatoni in a large pot of boiling water and drain.
5. Place rigatoni in a large flat casserole and mix it with the shrimp sauce.
6. Cut up the feta cheese and crumble it over the pasta.
7. Place under broiler until cheese is melted and slightly browned.

I often look at the menu offerings discussed in restaurant reviews. Many of them look delicious but, frankly, we would probably not get to sample too many of them. Either the restaurant is inaccessible or else, just too expensive. I do the next best thing; I try to figure out the recipe myself. Here is a recent and very good experiment if you're a cheese aficionado.

three cheese pasta **

- 2 tbsp. butter
- 1 cup heavy cream
- ¼ lb. gorgonzola cheese, crumbled
- ¼ lb. bel paesa cheese, shredded
- ½ lb. fontina cheese, shredded
- 1 lb. corkscrew pasta
- salt
- freshly ground black pepper
- ¾ cup grated parmesan cheese

1. In a large heavy pot, melt butter and put in ⅔ cup of cream.
2. When butter has melted in the cream, add the gorgonzola and stir over heat until mixed well.
3. Add the rest of the shredded cheeses and stir slowly until you have a nice creamy sauce.
4. Meanwhile, cook the pasta in a large pot of boiling, salted water and drain.
5. Add the pasta to the pot and mix thoroughly with the cheese sauce.
6. Add the rest of the cream, the salt and the pepper and mix again.
7. Serve with a bowl of parmesan on the side for those who want it.

Another recipe inspired by a menu, this one with salmon and dill is unusual.

italian salmon pasta **

- 3 tbsp. butter
- 6 tbsp. olive oil
- 2 cloves garlic, minced
- 1 8½ oz. can salmon, drained and well chopped
- 1½ to 2 cups light cream
- 2 tbsp. dill, chopped
- salt and pepper
- 1 lb. linguine
- grated parmesan cheese to serve on the side

1. Melt butter with 3 tbsp. of the olive oil in a large frying pan over low heat.
2. Add garlic and saute until golden.
3. Add salmon and cook for a few minutes, making sure the salmon is well chopped.
4. Slowly add cream until the sauce is well heated and of a nice consistency.
5. Stir in dill, salt and pepper.
6. In the meantime, cook linguine in a large pot of boiling water and drain.
7. Add the other 3 tbsp. olive oil to linguine and mix until linguine is well coated.
8. Pour sauce over linguine; mix again and serve with parmesan cheese on the side.

Our local Italian pork store is run by a man named Savario and it is one of my favorite stores because everything in it is so good. Savario grinds his own sausage, makes bracciole, various antipastos and even some of the cheeses. Best of all, he is always ready to tell you how to improve on your own Italian dishes, what to add, what to leave out and even how to experiment. Once he mentioned a particular salami that made a fine addition to pasta. So I went home and concocted this.

pasta with salami **

1 stick butter
1 lb. mushrooms, sliced
1½ cups mild salami, cut into small pieces
½ cup minced scallions
salt and pepper
3 egg yolks
1 cup heavy cream
½ cup grated parmesan cheese
1 lb. spaghetti

1. Melt butter in a heavy skillet and cook mushrooms over high heat until liquid has evaporated.
2. Lower heat, add salami, scallions, salt and pepper and cook for about 4 to 5 minutes.
3. In a separate bowl, beat eggs, cream, and cheese.
4. Meanwhile, cook pasta and drain.
5. Put pasta in serving bowl; add cream sauce and mix well.
6. Add salami sauce and mix well again.
7. Serve immediately with extra cheese on the side.

I love this pasta! I think that it looks pretty, it's easy to make and was served to me in a small unpretenious cafe in Italy, a pleasant surprise.

pasta with green beans **

1 lb. string beans, cut in two inch pieces
1 cup olive oil
1 cup bacon, minced
4 cloves garlic, minced
salt and pepper
½ cup olive oil
1 lb. fettuccine, green
3 tbsp. minced flat Italian parsley
1 cup grated parmesan cheese

1. Steam the green beans until tender.
2. Cook the bacon slowly until crisp, drain on paper towels and then crumble.
3. Saute beans, garlic, salt and pepper in olive oil for 3 minutes.
4. Add to cooked fettuccine along with bacon.
5. Sprinkle with parsley and parmesan and serve.

This is a lovely pasta, one of my favorites and so easy to make.

pasta with sausage *

1 lb. mild, sweet sausage
½ cup olive oil
⅔ cups scallion tops, minced
2 tbsp. raisins
salt and pepper
1 lb. taglionini (or other pasta such as corkscrews, ziti etc.)

1. With scissors, cut the casings away from the sausage and saute in the olive oil.
2. Chop the sausage into fine pieces as it cooks.
3. When meat is brown and well chopped, add the scallions, raisins, salt, and pepper and cook over low heat until scallions are tender and meat is completely cooked.
4. In the meantime, cook the taglionini and drain.
5. Add the parsley to the sausage and stir.
6. Pour sauce over the hot pasta, mix well, and serve.

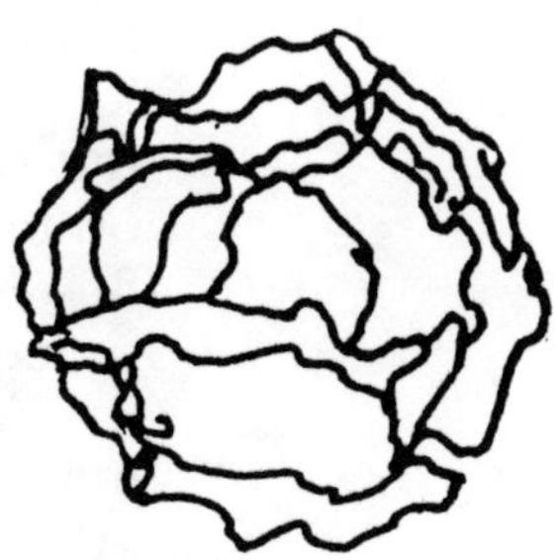

My husband and I visited Italy a few years ago and one of our most cherished memories is visiting the exquisite medieval town of San Gimignamo. It's hard to explain the feeling we had as we sat having a perfect lunch in a restaurant high on a mountain top overlooking lush vineyards. Food cooking in an open hearth, the snugness of being inside a small, walled village, a mist rising from the valley — all these things contributed to a lovely sense of continuity and pleasure. The food was superb and I have tried to approximate both our meals, not knowing now, in retrospect, how close I might have come, but the memories never change. Incidentally, the secret to this dish, I'm sure, is just coordination. Steps 7-10 should take only a minute.

san gimignamo pasta ***

- 4 tbsp. butter
- 2 tbsp. minced onions
- ½ lb. mushrooms, cleaned and cut in small pieces
- 1½ tsp. salt
- ¾ tsp. coarse, freshly ground black pepper
- ¾ cup minced, unsmoked ham
- ¾ cup peas, preferably small ones
- 1½ cups cream
- 1 lb. fettuccine
- ¾ cup grated parmesan cheese
- 1 egg, beaten

1. In a medium pan, melt 3 tbsp. of the butter and add onions, mushrooms, ¾ tsp. of the salt, pepper, and saute gently.
2. When you begin to see lots of liquid from the mushrooms, turn heat high and cook for 3 minutes.
3. Lower heat, add ham and peas and cook 1 minute.
4. Add ¾ cup of the cream and cook a couple of minutes more.
5. Put remaining butter and cream in a large serving dish and place in a 275 degree oven along with the pan containing the mushroom sauce.
6. Meanwhile, cook pasta according to directions and drain.
7. Take butter and cream sauce out of the oven and put on a very low flame on top of the stove.
8. Add pasta to butter and cream sauce and mix well.
9. Add cheese and beaten egg and mix well again.
10. Remove mushroom sauce from oven, add and give pasta a final mix.
11. Check for seasonings and serve immediately.

vegetables

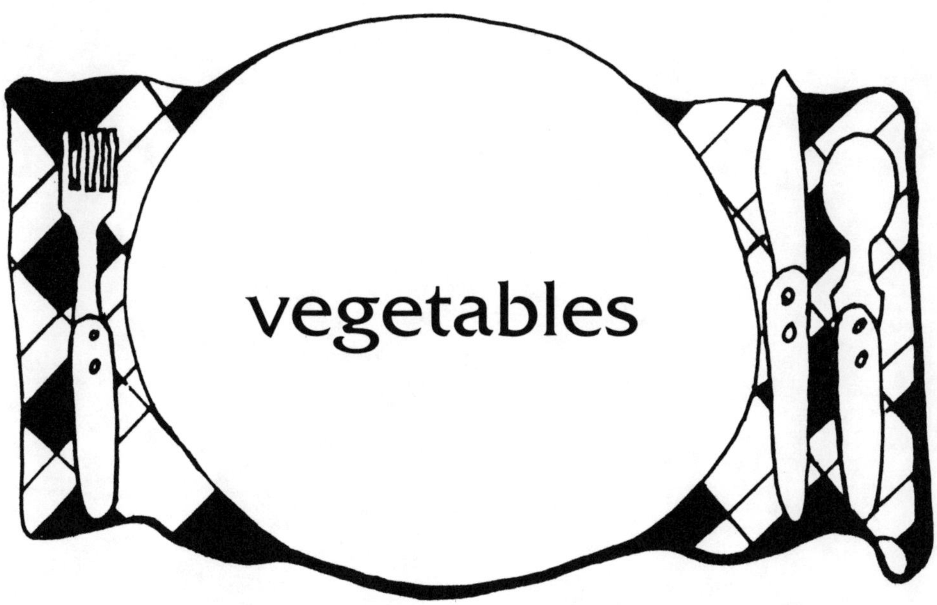

Marcia, my mother-in-law, has a wonderful way with cabbage and every time she visits us, she says, "If you have a little piece of cabbage I'll make something for you." This dish I loved and seemed to take no time at all. She said that she always cuts her cabbage with a knife and doesn't use a shredder. She advises tasting a lot and checking to see whether you want to add more sweet (sugar) or sour (lemon juice).

sweet and sour cabbage *

1 large onion, diced
1 medium cabbage, cut in chunks
1½ cups tomato puree
1½ cups water
2 tbsp. sugar
1 clove garlic, minced
juice from 1 lemon
1 tart, green apple, peeled and sliced
salt and pepper

1. Put all ingredients in a large frying pan or heavy pot and cook until cabbage is tender.

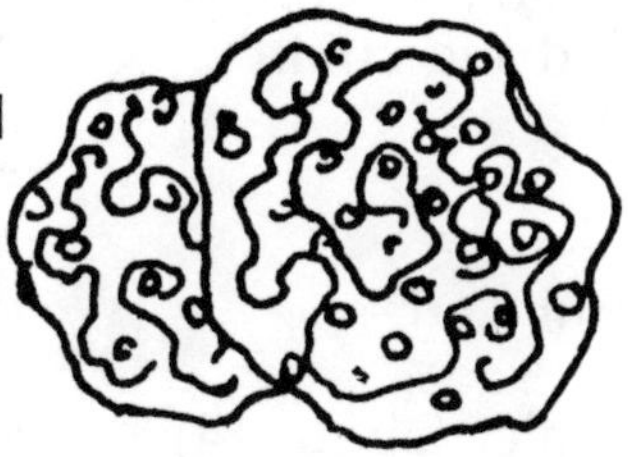

Another cabbage recipe, this one was donated by my friend, Chris Italiani who came for dinner one night when I was testing a very unsuccessful cabbage dish. She said, "I'll have my Mother send you her recipe. It's much better."

mrs. acheson's red cabbage *

2 tbsp. safflower oil
2 medium onions, chopped
½ head red cabbage, finely sliced
2 apples, peeled, cored and sliced
1 to 2 bay leaves
2 tbsp. vinegar
2 tbsp. brown sugar
½ cup water
salt and pepper

1. Saute onions in oil until transparent.
2. Add remaining ingredients and cook over low flame until cabbage is tender, approximately ½ hour.

One day I was looking for a new way to make eggplant. I happened to remember what Gene Friedman had said about his wife Dorothy's cooking. I had asked him why he thought she was such a good cook and one of the things he replied was "substitution." In other words, if she saw some nice turnips she might say, "Since I make potatoes au gratin, why not try turnips au gratin?" So, I decided, "Since I make a meat lasagna, why not make an eggplant lasagna?".

eggplant lasagna ***

1 eggplant cut in very small chunks
3 cloves garlic, sliced
1 medium onion, diced
6 tbsp. peanut oil
6 large tomatoes, skinned and chopped
1 green pepper, seeded and cut in strips
1½ cups tomato puree
1 basil leaf,minced
2 tbsp. fresh parsley, minced
salt and pepper
½ package lasagna noodles (about 14)
1 16-oz. package part skim mozzarella cheese, sliced
¾ cup grated parmesan cheese

1. Saute eggplant, garlic and onions in oil until eggplant is soft.
2. Add tomatoes, green pepper, puree, herbs and spices and cook over low heat for 40 minutes.
3. Meanwhile, cook lasagna noodles in large pot of boiling water and drain.
4. Take a large flat casserole and place half of the needles in bottom of dish.
5. Pour half of the eggplant tomato sauce over them and spread with half of the mozzarella cheese.
6. Layer with the rest of the noodles.
7. Pour the remaining sauce over them and then the rest of the mozzarella cheese.
8. Sprinkle parmesan over the casserole; cover with tinfoil and bake for 40 minutes in a 350 degree oven.
9. Take foil off and continue baking for 10 to 15 minutes more.

stuffed eggplant ***

3 small eggplants
2 small red peppers
6 tbsp. olive oil
1 large clove garlic, minced
salt and pepper
2 small onions, chopped
3 tomatoes, chopped
4 tbsp. minced fresh parsley
1 tsp. chopped fresh basil or ½ tsp. dried basil
½ cup wheat germ
¾ cup grated parmesan cheese
¼ cup chopped walnuts
2 tbsp. butter
¼ cup milk

1. Slice eggplants lengthwise and scoop out pulp.
2. Dice pulp.
3. Seed and dice red peppers.
4. Heat 3 tbsp. of the oil and saute eggplant and peppers and garlic until soft.
5. Add salt and pepper and divide mixture among eggplant shells, pressing it down to make room for the next ingredients.
6. Heat the rest of the oil and saute the onions, tomatoes, parsley, and basil until the onions are soft.
7. Spread this mixture on top of the eggplants.
8. Mix wheat germ, parmesan cheese and walnuts.
9. Melt butter over low heat in the milk.
10. Stir milk into wheat germ mixture to make a paste.
11. Spread on top of shells.
12. Place in oiled baking dish and cook in 350° oven for 45 minutes.

Esalen is a humanistic center for learning situated out in the Big Sur, a truly magnificent part of our country. The people at Esalen grow and cook all their own food high above the Pacific. The gardens are beautiful and I must say that the four days my husband and I spent there last year were four of the best eating experiences of our lives. Right after we came home, I tried to copy all the dishes we had had there.

I happen to like eggplant very much and make eggplant parmesan quite often, but that takes a lot of time.

I was pleased to find this recipe at Esalen. It takes much less time and is delicious. You may need to use more oil than I quoted. Eggplant seems to soak up so much of it. Also, you can try browning the eggplant by placing slices in an oiled baking pan and putting the pan in a hot oven.

esalen eggplant **

- 1 medium eggplant, sliced
- 2 eggs, beaten
- 1½ cups toasted breadcrumbs
- 1 cup peanut oil
- salt and pepper
- ¼ tsp. garlic salt
- 3 nice, good sized tomatoes, sliced
- ¾ cup grated parmesan cheese

1. Dip eggplant slices in egg and then in breadcrumbs.
2. Saute the slices in hot oil until brown and then turn over to brown on the other side.
3. Drain on paper towels and place in large flat baking dish.
4. Sprinkle with salt, pepper, and garlic salt.
5. Cover with tomato slices.
6. Sprinkle with parmesan cheese; cover with tinfoil and bake at 350 degrees for 40 minutes.

My Mother sent this to me and since I seem to be making lots of souffles these days, this seemed like a good one to include. Also, I had never heard of a souffle made with eggplant and this is very tasty.

mother's eggplant souffle **

1 large eggplant or two smaller ones, peeled and cubed
1 onion, thickly sliced
4 tbsp. butter
¼ cup bread crumbs
½ cup milk
3 egg yolks
¼ tsp. nutmeg
salt and pepper
3 egg whites
2 tbsp. breadcrumbs
2 tbsp. slivered almonds

1. Cook eggplant and onion in 2 cups of boiling water until tender. Discard onion.
2. Drain eggplant well and mash.
3. Add 2 tbsp. butter, breadcrumbs, milk, egg yolks, nutmeg, salt and pepper to eggplant and mix well.
4. Pour into a lightly buttered souffle dish and let cool.
5. When ready to bake, beat egg-whites until stiff and fold into eggplant mixture.
6. Saute breadcrumbs and almonds in the remaining 2 tbsp. butter for a few moments.
7. Sprinkle over souffle and bake in a 375 degree oven for 30 minutes.

Sue Mermelstein is a reporter for the East Hampton Star. A petite woman, bright and a terrific volleyball player, she took pity on us one night because we had been without a kitchen for two weeks and invited us for dinner. If you like eggplant and spiciness, this can't be beat.

sue's spicy eggplant **

2 tsp. Chinese chili paste with garlic
5 tsp. thin soy sauce
2 tsp. sugar
½ cup water
1 medium eggplant, cubed
4 tbsp. peanut oil
2 cloves garlic, sliced
1 large onion, cubed
4 cups rice, cooked

1. Mix chili paste, soy sauce, sugar, and water.
2. Heat oil in wok or large frying pan and stir fry eggplant until soft.
3. Remove eggplant, add garlic and stir fry for 1 minute.
4. Add onion and stir fry over lowered heat until soft.
5. Return eggplant to wok along with sauce and heat thoroughly before serv-serving over warm rice.

I saw eggplants something like these in that marvelous Italian case at Balducci's in New York City and came home to try and duplicate them. The inside of the eggplant should be saved, of course, and can be used in a variety of recipes.

ricotta eggplant **

4 baby eggplants
2 tbsp. olive oil
1 clove garlic, minced
1 small onion, diced
2 tbsp. chopped fresh parsley
1 basil leaf
½ tsp. oregano
salt and pepper
1 8-oz. can tomato puree
1 16-oz. carton of ricotta cheese
4 tbsp. grated parmesan cheese

1. Wash the eggplants; place on a cookie sheet and bake in 350 degree oven until a fork pierces them easily.
2. Remove from oven; slice lengthwise and cool.
3. Heat oil in a large frying pan and saute garlic and onion until golden.
4. Add the rest of the ingredients except the parmesan and ricotta cheese and simmer over a low heat for 20 minutes.
5. Scrape out eggplant pulp and save for another dish.
6. Place eggplant shells in a baking dish and divide the ricotta cheese among the eggplant shells.
7. Spoon tomato sauce over the shells.
8. Sprinkle with parmesan cheese and bake for 20 minutes in a 350 degree oven.

spinach provencale *

1 large onion, chopped
1 large clove garlic, minced
2 tbsp. olive oil
3 lbs. fresh washed spinach
2 eggs, beaten
¾ cups grated parmesan cheese
salt and pepper

1. Place onion and garlic in a large frying pan and saute in olive oil until soft.
2. Add spinach, cover and cook 4 minutes, or until spinach wilts.
3. Place spinach mixture on cutting board and chop.
4. When spinach has cooled, place in a buttered baking dish and stir in eggs, ½ cup of the parmesan cheese, salt and pepper.
5. Sprinkle with the remaining ¼ cup of cheese and bake at 375 degrees for 10 to 15 minutes.

I think this is probably my favorite squash dish and you can use butternut, or hubbard squash instead of acorn if you wish. You can also substitute sour cream for yogurt, but the yogurt's healthier, of course.

best ever squash *

2 nice sized acorn squashes
2 scallions, chopped
1 tbsp. butter
5 tbsp. yogurt
salt and pepper

1. Bake whole squashes until tender in a 350 degree oven (approximately 45 minutes to 1 hour).
2. When cooked, cut the squashes in half; carefully scrape out the pulp from the shells and reserve both squash and shells.
3. Saute scallions for a few minutes in butter.
4. Mash squash in bowl.
5. Add scallions, yogurt, salt and pepper and mix well.
6. Fill shells with the mixture and return to the oven to heat before serving.

Here's a nice pleasant complement to pasta or fish. Someone suggested that it is also served cold with the condiments when you are serving a curry dish.

string beans with almonds *

1 pound string beans
1 small package of slivered almonds
2 scallion tops, minced
3 tbsp. olive oil
salt and pepper
1 tbsp. vinegar

1. Steam whole string beans until tender, but not soft; drain.
2. Place in bowl with the almonds, scallions, oil, salt and pepper and mix well.
3. Add the vinegar and mix again.

What can one say about Minsky and still confine it to a few sentences? Richard Minsky is a master bookbinder, extraordinaire. The last book he bound was one that he wrote himself. It's called *Minsky in London* and sells for $1800. One is in the Victoria and Albert Museum, one in the rare books room of the New York Public Library, so you can see what kind of books they are. Richard himself is unique. He plays the violin and seems to have an informed opinion about everything topped with a good sense of humor. But as he says, "I'm just a regular guy." The following is a dish that he makes just about every night with variations. The variations depend on what's fresh at the market. I will give a standard recipe and you can substitute whatever is fresh, just as Minsky does.

minsky's vegetables **

2 large cloves garlic, minced
1 tsp. minced fresh ginger
3 tbsp. peanut oil
1 eggplant, cut in small cubes
1 large onion, sliced
1 cup celery, sliced
2 zucchini, sliced
2 carrots, shredded
1 tsp. cornstarch
2 tsp. water
2 tbsp. tamari
2 scallion tops cut in two inch pieces
4 cups cooked rice, brown or white

1. In a wok or large frying pan saute garlic and ginger in oil for a few minutes.
2. Add all the vegetables and stir fry until tender, but not mushy. (You will probably have to add more oil if you are using eggplant since it absorbs so much oil)
3. Dissolve cornstarch in water and add tamari.
4. Cook over low heat in a small saucepan until thickened.
5. Add to vegetables, cover, and heat through for a few minutes.
6. Serve over the rice with scallions sprinkled on top.

greek zucchini *

2 lbs. zucchini, sliced
2 large tomatoes, cut in chunks
1 medium onion, chopped
2 cloves garlic, minced
1 tsp. oregano
salt and pepper
3 tbsp. olive oil

1. Place all ingredients in a saucepan with a cover.
2. Cook over low heat until zucchini is tender.

Armand LaMacchia brought this to one of our communal meals. I thought it was a nice way to use parsnips as I don't have a great variety of recipes for them. I like the combination of these two vegetables.

armand's broccoli and parsnip casserole **

1 head of broccoli, trimmed and cut into stalks.
6 parsnips, peeled and sliced
2 tbsp. butter
2 tbsp. flour
¼ cup water
¾ cup milk
salt
¾ pound of sharp cheddar cheese, shredded.

1. Steam broccoli until crisp-tender.
2. Cook parsnips in a small amount of water.
3. Drain both vegetables.
4. Melt butter over low heat in a saucepan.
5. Make a flour and water paste and add to butter, stirring constantly.
6. Add milk gradually and stir until sauce is thickened.
7. Add salt and shredded cheese and keep stirring to make a nice cheese sauce.
8. Place vegetables in a casserole and cover with cheese sauce.
9. Bake covered for 30 minutes in a 350 degree oven.

The usual ways to prepare cauliflower are to steam it or, for the more ambitious, perhaps to bake it in a cheese sauce. This unusual dish can be served hot or cold and was given to me by a friend of a friend at one of our communal meals.

spicy cauliflower **

1 cauliflower, separated into flowerets
1 clove garlic, minced
1 tsp. peppercorns
3 tbsp. pine nuts
½ tsp. red pepper flakes
½ tsp. salt
¼ tsp. sugar
½ cup olive oil
¼ cup red wine vinegar

1. Steam cauliflower until crisp-tender.
2. Grind garlic, peppercorns, and pine nuts together; I use a mortar and pestle.
3. Place in a small bowl and add the red pepper flakes and sugar.
4. Add oil and mix thoroughly.
5. Pour sauce over cauliflower and stir well to coat.
6. Add vinegar last and mix all ingredients.

At our marvelous Italian pork store in East Hampton, which I have mentioned before, everything is made on the premises by the owners, Savario and his wife, Carmella. My husband got this recipe from him and as it came to him causally over the counter, the measurements are a little difficult and often depend on the size of the eggplant. Experiment!

savario's eggplant ***

1 long, narrow eggplant
3 eggs, beaten
1 cup flour
½ cup breadcrumbs
1 cup olive oil
3 cloves garlic
2 cups canned tomatoes, drained and chopped
¼ cup fresh basil or 1 tsp. dry basil
salt and pepper
8 oz. package mozzarella cheese
1 8 oz. carton ricotta cheese
2 cups fresh spinach, finely chopped

1. Skin eggplant and slice lengthwise into slices about 1 inch thick.
2. Dip eggplant into eggs.
3. Mix flour and breadcrumbs and coat each slice with the mixture.
4. Pour ⅔ cup of olive oil in a large flat casserole. You may have to use another dish because the eggplant shouldn't overlap.
5. Place eggplant in dish and cook in a 400 degree oven until done, turning once. This should take about half an hour. Drain on paper towels.
6. Put the remaining oil in a frying pan and saute garlic until golden.
7. Add tomatoes, basil, salt and pepper and cook over low heat for 20 minutes.
8. Slice mozzarella and mix with ricotta and spinach.
9. Place about 2 tbsp. of cheese mixture on end of each slice of eggplant and roll up so that it looks like a hot dog roll or manicotti.
10. Arrange in a smaller baking dish and cover with the tomato sauce.
11. Bake at 350 degrees for ½ hour.

My husband doesn't really like tofu, but I keep buying it because I think it's good for you and it's not expensive. I finally invented one dish that he liked and he said, "Quick, write it down for your next cookbook before you forget it."

tofu with apples *

1 tsp. fresh ginger, minced
2 large cloves garlic, minced
1 tbsp. safflower oil
1 large piece of tofu (around 8 oz.).
1 large apple, peeled and sliced
3 tbsp. tamari
2 scallions, slivered in two inch pieces

1. Saute ginger and garlic in oil for a few minutes, but do not let garlic brown.
2. Place tofu and apples in a small baking dish.
3. Add garlic, ginger and tamari.
4. Sprinkle with scallions, cover and bake at 350 degrees for ½ hour.

vegetable curry **

2 tbsp. salad oil
2 tsp. ground coriander
2 tsp. cumin
2 tsp. tumeric
¼ tsp. ground cloves
¼ tsp. cinnamon
3 garlic cloves, minced
¼ to ½ tsp. red pepper flakes
4 larges potatoes, peeled and cubed
2 cups chick peas
3 tomatoes, cut in chunks
1 larges green pepper, seeded and cut in strips
1½ cup peas
1½ tsp. salt
2 cups water
1½ cups yogurt
½ cup minced onion

1. Heat oil until hot and add garlic and spices.
2. Cook 2 minutes, stirring so it does not stick.
3. Add potatoes, chick peas, 2 of the tomatoes, green pepper and peas and mix well with the spices.
4. Add water and salt and heat until boiling. Reduce heat, cover and cook until potatoes are done.
5. Garnish with the remaining tomato and serve with yogurt mixed with onion.

I have wanted to include a recipe for soybeans because they are so healthy and they are inexpensive. I also think you have to cultivate a taste for them. I hope this helps. Remember to soak beans overnight first.

baked soybean casserole **

1 cup soybeans
3 tbsp. butter
1 small onion, chopped
1 small green pepper, sliced in thin strips
1 small red pepper, cut in strips
2 cloves garlic, sliced
½ tsp. thyme
2 tbsp. parsley
½ tsp. dill week
1 tbsp. safflower oil
3 tomatoes sliced
2 medium squashes, either yellow crookneck or zucchini, sliced in rounds.
½ cup grated parmesan cheese
salt and pepper to taste

1. Place beans in a large pot with 6 cups water and bring to a boil.
2. Cook 2 minutes, turn off heat, cover, and soak overnight.
3. In the morning, cook beans over low heat, uncovered, for about 2 to 3 hours or until done. Soybeans are usually slightly crunchy.
4. When done, drain, but reserve 1 cup of the cooking water.
5. Melt butter in a large skillet and saute onion, pepper, and garlic for a couple of minutes.
6. Add thyme, parsley, dill, soybeans and cooking water and cook over low heat for 15 minutes.
7. Grease a casserole with the safflower oil and add the soybeans along with tomatoes, squash, parmesan cheese, salt and pepper.
8. Mix well, cover, and bake at 300 degrees for 2 hours.

This sounds strange, but it's surprisingly good.

christina's geetam tofu steaks *

2 tbsp. tahini
2 tbsp. honey
6 tofu slabs, ¼ inch deep and cut into squares, 2 inches by 3 inches.
¼ cup tamari
3 tbsp. oil

1. Mix tahini, honey and tamari in a large flat pan.
2. Add tofu slabs and marinate for two hours.
3. Heat oil in large frying pan.
4. Fry tofu for a few minutes on each side.

green chilis with eggs and cheese *

3 cups grated Montery Jack or Swiss cheese
2 cans green chilis, drained and chopped
4 eggs, beaten

1. Pre-heat oven to 300 degrees.
2. Grease a square baking pan.
3. Add cheese to pan.
4. Sprinkle chopped chilis evenly over cheese.
5. Pour eggs into pan.
6. Bake 1 hour.
7. Cool and then cut into squares.

A quiche that is lighter than the usual kind, yogurt cheese pie is an interesting variation, has fewer calories and can be used with just about any kind of vegetables.

yogurt cheese pie **

½ cup grated Montery Jack cheese
½ cup grated cheddar cheese
1 unbaked pie shell
¼ cup onion, chopped
1 cup chopped vegetables, such as broccoli, cauliflower, zucchini, mushrooms, spinach etc.
4 eggs, beaten
½ cup cottage cheese
2 cups yogurt
½ cup milk
½ tsp. salt
½ tsp. white pepper
1 tsp. minced parsley
dash of cayenne

1. Mix the first two cheeses and place in the unbaked pie shell.
2. Add onions and vegetables to shell.
3. Mix remaining ingredients in a bowl.
4: Pour yogurt mixture into pie shell.
5. Bake at 350 degrees for 1 hour.

Spaghetti squash is a special favorite of a lot of my friends out here in the Hamptons. The only problem is that it is made with a squash called, appropriately enough, spaghetti squash and I don't know how readily available it is in other parts of the country. It is a large, pale yellow squash. When it is baked and cut open, the strands are scraped out and look very much like spaghetti strands. I suppose that if you can't find this type of squash, you can use Dorothy Friedman's maxim and substitute another type of squash and use the sauce over it.

spaghetti squash with tomato sauce **

1 good sized spaghetti squash
2 cloves garlic, minced
1 small green pepper, seeded and minced
1 celery stalk, cut in small pieces
2 tbsp. olive oil
6 large tomatoes, skinned and cut in pieces
2 tbsp. tomato paste
⅓ cup water
1 tsp. minced fresh basil
salt and pepper
¼ tsp. red pepper flakes
1 cup grated parmesan cheese

1. Place the squash in a pan with a tiny bit of water in the bottom and bake at 350 degrees until done. This may take an hour to an hour and a half depending on the size of the squash. A fork should puncture it easily.
2. While the squash is cooking, saute the garlic, green pepper, and celery in the olive oil.
3. When garlic is lightly colored, add remaining ingredients except for cheese and simmer for about 1 hour.
4. When squash is done, cut it open, take out seeds and gently scoop out squash strands with a fork.
5. Pour the tomato sauce over the squash and serve with the parmesan cheese on the side.

stuffed tomatoes **

- 4 good sized, ripe tomatoes
  salt and pepper
- 1 clove garlic, minced
- 3 tbsp. minced scallions
- 3 tbsp. minced parsley
- 1 tsp. fresh basil or ¼ tsp. dried basil
- ⅓ tsp. thyme
- ½ cup fresh bread crumbs
- 3 tbsp. olive oil
- 2 tbsp. butter

1. Cut the tomatoes in half horizontally.
2. Scoop out the seeds and pulp and save for soups or sauces.
3. Sprinkle the tomato shells with salt and pepper and turn over to drain.
4. Combine the remaining ingredients, except butter.
5. When you are ready to cook the tomatoes, pre-heat the oven to 400 degrees.
6. Fill the shells with the breadcrumb mixture, dot with butter and bake in a lightly greased flat baking pan for 15 minutes.

broccoli frittata **

- 6 large cloves garlic, sliced
- 3 tbsp. olive oil
- 1 medium head broccoli, trimmed and chopped in small pieces.
- 6 eggs, well beaten
- ½ cup parmesan cheese
  salt and pepper, to taste
- 3 tbsp. butter

1. Saute garlic in olive oil until almost golden.
2. Add chopped broccoli and stir fry a few minutes until broccoli is coated with oil.
3. Add ¼ cup of water, cover, lower heat and simmer until broccoli is tender. Drain all liquid off.
4. In a bowl, mix the broccoli with eggs, parmesan cheese, salt and pepper.
5. Melt butter in a large frying pan.
6. Pour egg/broccoli mixture in frying pan and cover.
7. Cook until eggs are set.
8. Place pan under broiler and cook until the frittata is nicely browned on top.
9. Cut in pie shaped wedges and serve hot or cold.

turnip casserole *

- 6 cups turnips or rutabaga, peeled and cubed
- ½ tsp. salt
- ¼ tsp. caraway seeds
- 2 tsp. fresh basil or ½ tsp. dried basil
- ¼ cup lemon juice
- 1 cup yogurt
- freshly ground black pepper
- 2 tbsp. minced parsley

1. Steam turnips until tender and put into a casserole.
2. Mix salt, caraway seeds, basil, lemon juice and yogurt.
3. Pour over turnips and sprinkle with black pepper and parsley.
4. Bake, covered, in a 375 degree oven for 20 minutes.

Anna Marie Frisbee is a friend who lives out here in the Hamptons. She has a lovely face, a good sense of humor and is struggling to care for her very active young son, Matthew, who I'm sure doesn't give her much time to cook. However, she is very conscious of preparing healthy foods, as the following recipe for a delicious quiche will attest.

anna marie's spinach quiche ***

- 4 tbsp. butter
- 3 tbsp. wholewheat flour
- 1¼ cups milk
- 2 tbsp. soy sauce
- ¼ cup white wine
- 3 tbsp. chopped parsley
- 4 eggs (at room temperature)
- 1 cup well packed grated cheddar cheese
- 1 medium onion, chopped
- ¾ cup sliced mushrooms
- 3 tbsp. oil
- 3 cups chopped spinach
- 2 8-inch pie shells
- a few grindings of fresh nutmeg

1. Melt butter over low heat and add flour.
2. Slowly add the milk, a little at a time and cook for 5 minutes, stirring constantly so the sauce doesn't get lumpy.
3. Cool slightly and then add soy sauce, wine, and parsley.
4. When it is cool, add one egg at a time, stirring after each addition.
5. Add cheese, stir and set aside.
6. In a wok or large frying pan, saute onions and mushrooms for 4 or 5 minutes in the oil.
7. Add spinach, tossing just until it starts to wilt.
8. Combine spinach with cheese sauce.
9. Prick the bottoms of the pie shells and place in a pre-heated 400 degree oven for five minutes.
10. Turn heat down to 350 degrees.
11. Divide spinach-cheese mixture between the two shells.
12. Grate a little nutmeg over the tops.
13. Bake the quiches for 35 to 45 minutes or until a knife inserted into the center comes out clean.

When we were at Esalen and this dish was posted on the bulletin board as part of the evening menu, everyone groaned. Later they all went back for seconds, so don't write it off. Actually, you could probably use other types of greens, such as spinach, collard greens etc. successfully.

swiss chard cutlets **

3 cups coarsely chopped swiss chard
¼ cup chopped onion
¼ cup breadcrumbs
½ cup grated parmesan cheese
2 eggs
2 tbsp. lemon juice
salt and pepper
2 tbsp. oil

1. Steam Swiss chard until tender.
2. Place all ingredients in blender and blend slightly.
3. Heat oil in a large frying pan and when it is hot, pour the mixture on the hot griddle as if you were making pancakes. Make sure they are nicely browned before you flip them over.

My sister-in-law Linda made this for us and I adopted it. A nice easy quiche to make, I like to prepare some extra ones to have on hand in the freezer. You can use a prepared pie shell to save time.

linda's easy quiche **

1⅓ cups flour
1 stick butter, softened
1 cup heavy cream
1½ tsp. sugar
2 eggs
⅓ tsp. cayenne pepper
8 oz. Swiss cheese, shredded
1 cup thinly sliced onion

1. Mix flour and butter and press into a pie pan.
2. Mix cream, sugar, eggs, and pepper in the blender for only 30 seconds.
3. Put cheese and onions in the unbaked pie shell.
4. Pour the cream mixture over the cheese and onions and bake for 20 minutes in a 425 degree oven.
5. Lower heat to 350 degrees and bake for another 30 minutes.

We have a lot of beautiful white and purple cauliflower piled up in great mounds along with the pumpkins at roadside stands in the fall out here in the Hamptons. When a friend remarked that she never quite knew what to do with cauliflower except cover it with a cheese sauce, I tried to come up with a new dish for her.

italian cauliflower *

1 medium head of cauliflower, trimmed and broken into flowerets.
1 pound of pasta (rigatoni, shells or bows)
½ cup olive oil
1 tsp. minced garlic
3 tbsp. chopped parsley
salt and pepper
1 cup grated cheese
sprinkling of red pepper flakes

1. Steam cauliflower until tender and drain.
2. While cauliflower is steaming, cook pasta in boiling water until *al dente*; drain.
3. Saute garlic and parsley in olive oil until garlic turns slightly golden.
4. Place cauliflower and pasta in serving bowl and pour the olive oil with garlic and parsley over it.
5. Add salt, pepper, grated cheese and mix well.
6. Sprinkle with a small amount of red pepper flakes and serve.

It probably goes without saying that I only put dishes in this book that I like. In compiling the recipes, some stand out in my mind as being extra special. This stuffed zucchini comes from Judy Wolfe's friend Carlos, a person I don't even know. Delicious!

carlos' stuffed zucchini ***

4 medium zucchini
¾ cup chopped onion
1 clove garlic, minced
¾ cup skinned and chopped tomatoes
½ cup chopped mushrooms
½ cup breadcrumbs
2 tbsp. chopped capers
3 tbsp. minced parsley
2 leaves fresh basil, minced
salt and pepper
½ cup olive oil

1. Steam zucchini over boiling water for 4 minutes.
2. Slice zucchini in half lengthwise and scoop out pulp.
3. Chop zucchini pulp into small pieces and place in bowl.
4. Add all the remaining ingredients with the exception of the olive oil. Add only ¼ cup of the oil and mix well.
5. Place zucchini shells in a large slightly oiled baking dish and stuff with the filling.
6. Drizzle the remaining olive oil over the zucchini shells and bake in a 350 degree oven for ½ hour.

christina's cauliflower and tomato special *

1 small onion, chopped
1 small cauliflower, trimmed and broken into small flowerets
4 tbsp. tomato puree
3 medium sized tomatoes, chopped
1½ tsp. rosemary
1 tsp. oregano
½ tsp. garlic salt
salt and freshly ground black pepper
2 tbsp. tamari

1. Lightly saute onion in oil.
2. Add cauliflower and saute a few minutes more.
3. Add all remaining ingredients and mix thoroughly.
4. Cover and and cook over low heat, stirring occasionally until cauliflower is done, but not mushy.

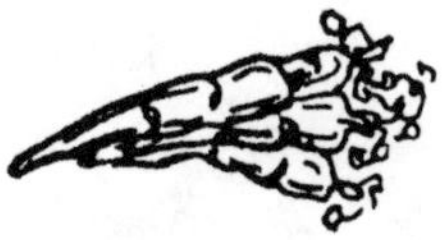

This is another one from my mother-in-law, Marcia, volunteered enthusiastically. It is a dish that can be made with either squash or corn.

marcia's squash or corn souffle *

2 cups yellow crookneck squash, cut in small cubes. (See note.)
2 tbsp. melted butter
2 tbsp. sugar
¼ tsp. salt
2 eggs, beaten
½ cup flour
1 cup milk

1. Cook squash in a small amount of boiling water until tender, but not mushy; drain.
2. Melt butter in an ovenproof casserole.
3. Add sugar, salt and eggs to dish.
4. Stir in flour and milk.
5. Add squash; stir and bake 1 hour in a 350 degree oven.

Note: If you wish to make a corn souffle, substitute 1 cup of creamed corn for squash and use only 1 tbsp. sugar.

This dish was given to me by Christina, an Australian lady we met at one of our communal meals. I have a dessert recipe of hers in the dessert section that is probably one of my all-time favorites. But this is healthier.

christina's rice and spinach casserole **

- ½ cup sunflower seeds (sesame seeds can be substituted)
- 2 tbsp. butter
- 2 cups tomato sauce or juice
- 1 pound fresh spinach, cooked and well chopped
- 6 cups cooked brown rice
- ½ tsp. oregano
- ½ tsp. thyme
- 4 oz. hard cheddar cheese, grated
- ¾ tsp. paprika

1. Saute sunflower seeds or sesame seeds lightly in butter for a few minutes.
2. Mix tomato sauce with spinach, rice, oregano, and thyme and simmer until most of the liquid is absorbed.
3. Add the seeds and mix well.
4. Place in a baking dish and sprinkle with the cheese and paprika.
5. Bake for 30 minutes at 375 degrees.

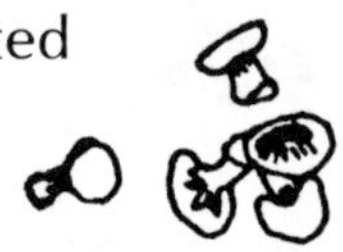

Christina is a disciple of the Indian guru, Rajneesh and is now living on one of his ashrams in Vermont. One day I received in the mail a package of recipes from her to test for my book. Mushroom Special is a very nice and different way to use mushrooms. Her recipe called for sour cream. I used yogurt. Both work nicely.

mushroom special **

- 3 tbsp. sesame seeds
- 3 medium onions, sliced and separated into rings
- 2 tbsp. butter
- ⅔ cup sour cream or yogurt
- 2 tbsp. tahini
- 1 tbsp. tamari
- ½ tsp. celery salt
- ½ tsp. black pepper
- ½ lb. mushrooms, sliced
- 3 sticks celery, sliced in small pieces
- ½ cup raisins

1. Toast sesame seeds lightly in a frying pan and set aside.
2. In a good sized frying pan, lightly fry the onions in butter and remove to a plate.
3. Mix sour cream or yogurt, tahini, tamari, celery salt, and pepper.
4. Add remaining ingredients to the frying pan and stir in the yogurt sauce.
5. Simmer over low heat, stirring occasionally.
6. Add onions and heat a few minutes more.
7. Put in serving dish and sprinkle sesame seeds on top.

Marty's cousin Cynthia whipped something like this up so quickly one night that I felt I certainly should include it, especially because I think that chickpeas are a good staple.

cynthia epstein's easy chickpea stew *

2 tbsp. safflower oil
1 large onion, sliced
1 green pepper, chopped
1 clove garlic, minced
1 lb. 12 oz. can tomatoes
1 20 oz. can chickpeas, drained
1 tbsp. curry powder
½ tsp. chili powder
1 tsp. oregano
salt and pepper

1. In the oil, saute onions, green pepper, and garlic until onions are golden.
2. Add tomatoes, chickpeas and spices; cover and cook over low heat for 20 minutes.

sesame asparagus *

2 lbs. asparagus, cut and trimmed into 2-inch pieces
2 tbsp. safflower oil
1 tbsp. dark sesame oil
1 tbsp. lemon juice
1 tbsp. sesame seeds

1. Heat safflower oil in wok or heavy frying pan.
2. Add asparagus and stir fry over high heat for a couple of minutes, so that asparagus is well coated with oil
3. Lower heat; add 2 tbsp. water; cover and cook until asparagus is done. It should be crunchy. Do not overcook.
4. Transfer to serving bowl and toss with sesame oil.
5. Add lemon juice; stir and sprinkle with sesame seeds.

meat

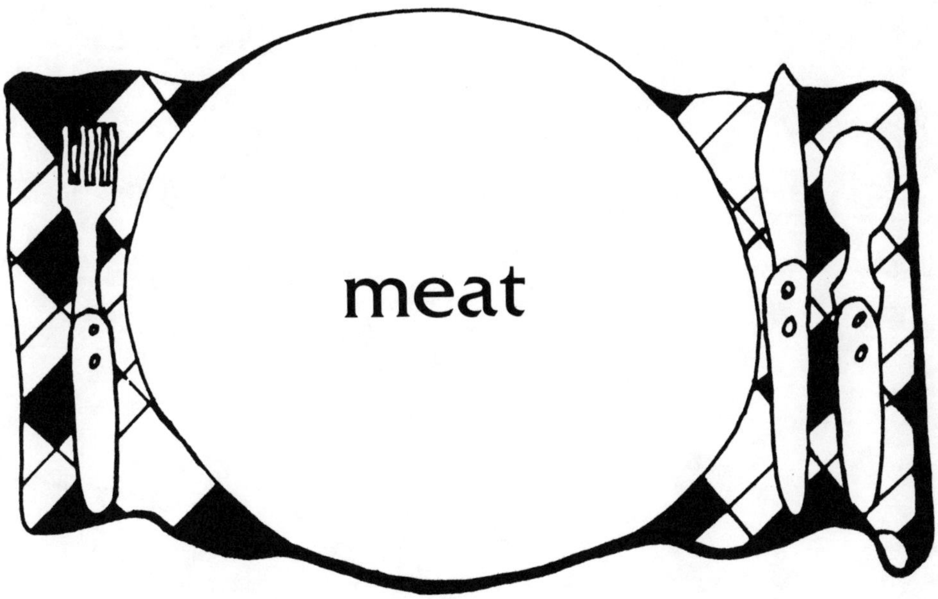

short rib stew ***

4 lbs. lean short ribs, cut in 3-inch pieces
2 medium onions, chopped
½ cup chopped carrots
3 cups rich beef broth
½ tsp. marjoram
1 tsp. caraway seeds
1 bay leaf
½ tsp. savory
1½ tsp. salt
1 tsp. pepper
grated rind of one lemon
¼ cup wine vinegar
3 tbsp. whole wheat flour
¼ cup water
¾ lb. mushrooms, sliced
1 small green pepper cut in thin strips
2 tbsp. oil

1. Heat a shallow roasting pan in a 500 degree oven for 5 minutes.
2. Put ribs in pan and brown for about 15 minutes, turning in order to brown all sides.
3. Transfer ribs to a large heavy pot; lower heat to 350 degrees and cook for 30 minutes.
4. Pour off fat; place pot on top of stove; add onions and carrots and cook until onions are transparent.
5. Add beef broth, seasoning, grated lemon, and vinegar.
6. Cover, put back in oven and cook for 1½ hours.
7. Make a paste of the flour and water and cook on top of the stove until thick.
8. Add to stew in oven.
9. Saute mushrooms and peppers in oil until tender.
10. Add to stew and cook 15 minutes more.

For anyone who loves sauerkraut as I do, this goulash is a must. I happen to use a pork tenderloin, but a less expensive cut of meat such as pork shoulder will do. It takes about 2½ to 3 hours, so give yourself enough time.

company goulash ***

3 slices of bacon
2 cloves garlic, minced
2 large onions, sliced
2 cans (1 lb., 15 oz.) sauerkraut, rinsed and drained
2 tbsp. caraway seeds
14 peppercorns
6 juniper berries, bruised
1 cup white wine
2 cups chicken broth
2 tbsp. oil
3 lbs. pork tenderloin cut in cubes
2 tbsp. paprika
1 1 lb., 12-oz. can tomatoes
salt and pepper, to taste
1 cup sour cream
1 tbsp. grated lemon rind

1. Slowly cook bacon until almost done.
2. Pour off all but 3 tbsp. grease; add garlic and onions and cook until soft.
3. Add sauerkraut, stir and cook for a few minutes.
4. Pour into large casserole and add caraway seeds, peppercorns, juniper berries, wine and chicken broth.
5. Cover and cook in a 325 degree oven for 1 hour.
6. Sprinkle pork with paprika and brown in a frying pan in the 2 tbsp. oil.
7. Add pork, canned tomatoes, salt and pepper to sauerkraut; stir well, cover, and return to oven for another hour and a half.
8. Stir in sour cream, sprinkle with lemon peel and serve.

I happen to like dishes from Thailand, Vietnam, and Indonesia very much. We have a favorite Thai restaurant in New York and have often tried to inquire about the recipes for certain dishes. The owner is charming, but doesn't speak English well, so we're not very successful. This particular dish was given to me by a friend who knew that I liked this type of food. It's quite unusual, I think.

mary's pork sate ***

4 teaspoons small walnut pieces
1 medium onion, minced
1 tbsp. grated ginger
2 cloves of garlic, minced
juice from 1 lemon or lime
salt and pepper
1½ lb. lean, boneless pork, cut in cubes

1. Blend all ingredients except pork.
2. Mix pork cubes with this marinade and marinate for at least 4 hours.
3. Broil pork on a charcoal grill or under the broiler until done.
4. Serve with dipping sauce. (I think this sauce could be used with all kinds of meat.)

Dipping Sauce

¾ cup roasted peanuts
2 tbsp. peanut oil
2 scallions, slivered
½ tsp. dried chilis
1 small onion, minced
½ tsp. salt
boiling water
1½ tbsp. tamari
juice of 1 lime or lemon

1. Grind the peanuts in a blender.
2. In the oil, saute the slivered scallions for 2 minutes.
3. Add chili and onion and fry 2 minutes more.
4. Place mixture in a bowl and add peanuts and salt.
5. Add enough boiling water to make a smooth paste.
6. Stir in the tamari and lemon or lime juice and serve in a dipping bowl.

pork chops with raisin stuffing **

6 nice sized pork chops
2 tbsp. oil
½ tsp. pepper
3 cups toasted bread crumbs
1½ cups chopped peeled apples
½ cup raisins
½ cup celery
½ cup onions
½ tsp. poultry seasoning
¼ tsp. pepper
1 cup beef or vegetable broth
3 tart red apples, cored and halved

1. Brown chops slowly on both sides in oil.
2. Place in a heavy baking dish and sprinkle with ¼ tsp. pepper.
3. Combine bread crumbs, chopped apples, raisins, celery, onions, poultry seasoning and the other ¼ tsp. pepper.
4. Add broth and mix well.
5. Spread stuffing evenly over pork chops.
6. Lay 1 apple half on top of each pork chop.
7. Cover with foil or a lid and bake in a 350 degree hour for 1 hour.

My husband and I stopped in Portofino, Italy and were very fortunate to find not only a lovely pension to stay in, but one that was presided over by a superb and joyous cook. His son waited on us for dinner. We were the only guests as it was off-season, so his father went off happily to prepare something for us. When we praised the meal to his son, our waiter, the young son proudly replied, "If you like this, you should taste my Father's cooking when he really cooks." I have tried to approximate our main dish. I have experimented with it a number of times and this is as close as I can get.

portofino pork with sauce ***

4 to 5 lb. pork loin
fresh black pepper
1 tsp. oregano
1 tbsp. minced parsley
2 cloves garlic, crushed
1 cup white wine
2 cups water

1. Preheat oven to 400 degrees.
2. Put pork in roasting pan and sprinkle with pepper, oregano, and parsley.
3. Roast in oven for ½ hour.
4. Add garlic, wine and water, cover and reduce heat to 350 degrees; cook for 1½ hours or until pork is done, basting occasionally.
5. Slice meat and spoon sauce over each serving.

Sauce

2 tbsp. olive oil
2 tbsp. onion, finely chopped
½ cup carrots, cut into very fine julienne strips, about 2 inches long
½ cup celery, cut into very fine julienne strips, about 2 inches long
⅓ tsp. thyme
salt and pepper
¼ cup white wine
¼ cup water
a few tbsp. sauce from roasting meat near the end of it's roasting time (to add flavor)

1. In the oil, saute onions, carrots, and celery for a few minutes.
2. Add spices, wine and water.
3. Cover, turn heat low and cook until done. The carrots and celery should be very soft.
4. Toward the end of the cooking time, add two to three tbsp. of broth from the roasting pan to add flavor.

Athos Zacharias is a fine painter who lives in New York and the Hamptons. For years now, he has been working on a house which he built himself and it is becoming as much a work of art as his paintings. Recently, we went to his home for dinner and to consider which of five paintings we were going to purchase. Our mutual friend, Richard Minsky had also been invited. The evening was prepared with great care — the dinner, the viewing of the paintings, and the four of us playing a little music on assorted instruments afterwards. One of the highlights, however, was Zach's shy announcement that he had created a new meatloaf for my second cookbook. Zach has come newly to cooking, so I was a little apprehensive. It's hard to turn a friend's dish down. To my delight and surprise, it was wonderful, pretty to look at, delicious to eat, unlike the usual meatloaves, and a tribute to Zach's everpresent creativity.

zach's mint meatloaf **

3 tbsp. butter
2 large white onions, chopped fine
2 cloves garlic, minced
2 lbs. ground chuck
2 eggs, beaten
¼ cup water
¾ cups Italian bread crumbs
2 sweet red peppers, chopped fine
½ tsp. tarragon
½ generous cup of minced fresh mint or 3 level tsp. dried mint (if fresh is unavailable)
salt and pepper
⅓ cup wheat germ
4 tsp. honey

1. In the butter, saute onions and garlic until soft.
2. Place ground chuck in a mixing bowl and add the onions and garlic.
3. Add eggs, water, bread crumbs, sweet peppers, tarragon, mint, salt, and pepper; mix well with your hands.
4. Place ingredients in a baking dish and shape into a nice loaf.
5. Sprinkle wheat germ on top and drizzle honey over the wheat germ. (Zach wrote that one should drizzle the honey in an interesting pattern. Why not?)
5. Bake in a 350 degree oven for about 1 hour.

Ginger beef stew is one of the those recipes that I have found along the way and I have not the slightest idea where it came from. My husband suggested a variation as he likes vegetarian meals.

ginger beef stew **

4 medium onions, chopped fine
4 cloves garlic, minced
1 tsp. salt
1 tsp. tumeric
½ tsp. crushed chili pepper
2 tsp. grated fresh ginger
1 flank steak or an equally good cut of beef
½ cup sesame oil
2 cups chopped tomatoes
2 cups beef broth

1. Mix the first six ingredients.
2. If you are using flank steak, cut it in 4-inch strips. If you are using another kind of beef, cut it in small cubes.
3. Marinate the meat in the spices for 3 hours.
4. Heat sesame oil in large frying pan and brown meat quickly.
5. Add tomatoes and beef broth.
6. Lower heat, cover and stew until meat is tender.

Marty's Variation **

1. Instead of using flank steak, peel and cube a large eggplant.
2. Coat the eggplant with the first six ingredients. You do not need to marinate the eggplant for any amount of time.
3. Heat the oil and brown the eggplant.
4. Add only 1 cup of beef broth with the tomatoes, turn heat down, cover and simmer until tender.

A marvelous dish from Judy Wolfe's friend Carlos again. Every recipe of his has been especially good.

carlos' liver and noodle casserole **

½ lb. chicken livers
½ lb. mushrooms, sliced
3 tbsp. butter
½ pint sour cream
¼ cup dry white wine
1 lb. noodles (any size or kind)
½ cup minced parsley
3 tbsp. chives
⅓ cup grated parmesan cheese

1. Saute chicken livers and mushrooms in butter until livers are brown on the outside.
2. Stir in sour cream, wine, salt and pepper and mix well.
3. Meanwhile, cook noodles in boiling water until *al dente*; drain.
4. Place noodles and liver/mushroom mixture in a casserole and mix well.
5. Sprinkle parsley, chives, and parmesan cheese on top.
6. Cover with lid or foil and bake in a 350 degree oven for 20 to 25 minutes.

My mother must have given me this recipe at least 25 years ago and after I typed this, the original paper simply fell apart. Since veal is so terribly expensive, my husband suggested chicken cutlets, a perfectly acceptable substitute. If you use chicken, of course, you must cook it a little longer than veal.

scallopini lucia **

6 tbsp. butter
½ lb. mushrooms, thinly sliced
½ cup boiling water
½ cup white wine
⅛ tsp. freshly ground nutmeg
¾ cup flour
salt and pepper
2 tbsp. tomato paste
¼ cup sour cream

1. Melt 3 tbsp. butter and saute mushrooms for 5 minutes.
2. Add the boiling water, wine and nutmeg and let simmer 20 minutes.
3. Lightly coat the veal with flour, salt and pepper and saute in the other 3 tbsp. butter until light brown. This takes only a few minutes or the veal will turn tough.
4. Add the juices from the veal pan to the mushroom sauce along with the tomato paste.
5. Simmer 5 minutes longer.
6. Add the veal slices and the sour cream and simmer just a few seconds until hot.
7. Serve immediately.

Judy Wolfe said to me wonderingly, "What, you've never heard of picadillo?. Come over to my house next week and I'll make it for you." We did indeed go over and eat picadillo. I liked it and thought that perhaps if I hadn't heard of it, some other enthusiastic cooks might not know about it either.

judy wolfe's picadillo **

½ cup raisins or currents
2 tbsp. peanut oil
1 large onion, finely chopped
2 cloves garlic, minced
1 large green pepper, seeded and chopped finely
1 cup stuffed green olives
1 3 oz. jar capers
2 tbsp. vinegar
salt and pepper
½ tsp. cinnamon
¼ tsp. allspice
1 bay leaf
a dash of tabasco sauce
2 lbs. ground meat
1 16-oz. can tomatoes, partially drained.
½ cup chili sauce

1. Place raisins or currants in a bowl of warm water so that they will "plump up."
2. Heat 1 tbsp. of the oil in a frying pan, add onions, garlic, and green pepper and cook until soft.
3. Add olives, capers, vinegar, salt, pepper, spices, bay leaf, and tabasco sauce and cook 5 minutes.
4. Cook ground meat separately in a skillet until it just loses its pink color.
5. Pour off any grease and add the olive and spice mixture to the ground meat, stirring to blend.
6. Drain raisins and add.
7. Add tomatoes and chili sauce and cook over low heat for about 45 minutes.
8. Serve with saffron rice, sour cream and chopped hard boiled egg as Judy does, if you wish.

A perfect dish to make in chilly weather, choucroute garnie is a rather well known dish and everyone must have a favorite recipe. It is simply various cuts of pork and sausages baked with sauerkraut and either juniper berries or gin to give it a special flavor. You can substitute other kinds of pork from what I have used in this dish if you wish.

choucroute garnie **

- 2 large onions, chopped
- 1 large carrot, chopped
- 3 tbsp. peanut oil
- 1 large clove garlic, minced
- 2 tart apples, peeled, cored, and chopped
- 2 1 lb., 11-oz. cans sauerkraut
- 2½ cups chicken broth
- 1 cup dry white wine
- 1 bay leaf
- 8 whole peppercorns
- 8 juniper berries or 2 tbsp. gin
- salt and pepper
- 1½ lb. kielbasa sausage, cut in three inch pieces
- ½ lb. baked ham, sliced
- 1½ lbs. boneless smoked pork tenderloin, sliced

1. In a large frying pan, saute onion and carrots until soft.
2. Add garlic and apple and saute a few minutes more.
3. In the meantime, drain sauerkraut and rinse with cold water.
4. Add to pan along with chicken broth and wine.
5. When the stew begins to simmer, add the bay leaf, peppercorns, juniper berries or gin, salt and pepper and stir well.
6. Transfer to a large deep baking dish, cover, and bake at 325 degrees for 2 hours.
7. Add kielbasa and cook 20 minutes more. If broth has evaporated, add more broth or wine.
8. Add the ham and pork, cover and cook 20 minutes more.
9. Serve with hot mustard.

When I was a newlywed, I complained that although chicken livers were cheap and fit my budget, I didn't like them. A neighbor from upstairs said, "Nonsense, you just don't know how to prepare them and I will show you how." He did — so here they are. I really did like them, much to my surprise.

al maline's chicken livers *

3 tbsp. olive oil
2 cloves garlic, minced
1 cup sliced onions
1 cup green pepper, sliced
1 pound chicken livers, trimmed and cut in pieces
½ tsp. rosemary
½ cup white wine
salt and lots of pepper

1. In the oil, saute garlic for a few minutes.
2. Add onions and peppers and saute a few minutes more.
3. In the meantime, pat the chicken livers dry and add to the frying pan. Cook until almost done.
4. Turn heat low and add the rosemary, wine, salt and pepper.
5. Cover and cook for five minutes.

My husband says this is his favorite way to prepare liver. It couldn't be simpler.

calves liver with lemon *

1 lb. calves liver
⅓ cup flour
2 tbsp. butter
2 tbsp. oil
juice from 2 lemons
2 tbsp. finely chopped fresh parsley

1. Trim liver well and cut in thin strips.
2. Dredge liver on both sides lightly in the flour.
3. Heat butter and oil in a skillet and, when hot, saute liver until done, turning once. It should be brown on the outside, but still pink inside.
4. Remove to serving platter.
5. Add lemon juice and parsley to pan and for 1 minute scrape the sides and bottom of the pan well with a wooden spoon.
6. Pour sauce over liver and serve immediately.

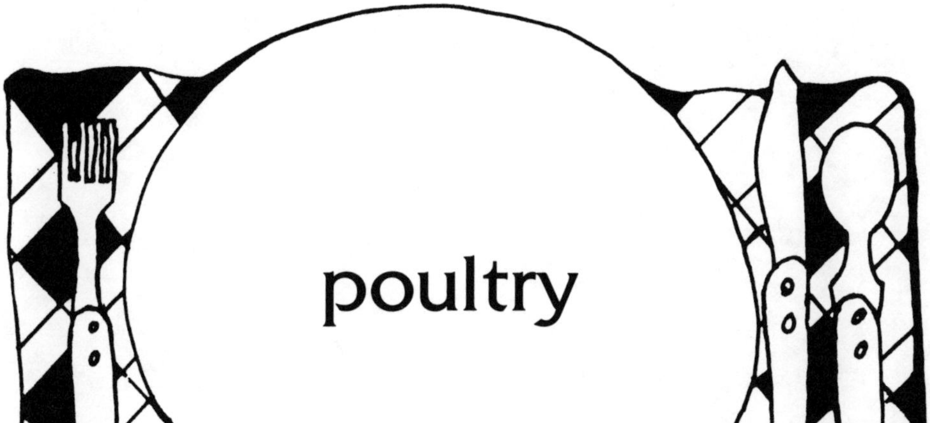

poultry

An easy baked chicken recipe given to me by Mrs. Feiman when I was first married, this seems to please children everywhere, and adults have no complaints either. You can purchase cornflake crumbs, but I prefer to buy my own cornflakes in a health food store and grind them in my blender.

mrs. feiman's baked chicken *

- ¼ cup safflower oil
- ¼ tsp. salt
- ¼ tsp. garlic salt
- ½ tsp. pepper
- 1 frying chicken, cut in pieces
- 2 cups cornflakes crumbs

1. Mix oil, salt, garlic salt, and pepper in a small dish.
2. With a pastry brush, coat each piece of chicken with seasoned oil.
3. Dip chicken pieces in cornflake crumbs and place in a lightly greased flat baking dish, making sure that pieces don't overlap.
4. Cover with foil and bake for 45 minutes in a 350 degree oven.
5. Remove foil and bake 15 minutes more until chicken is brown and crisp.

The only dish I know from Pakistan, this spicy chicken has a unique flavor.

pakistani chicken *

- 4 chicken breasts
- 6 cloves garlic, minced
- 2 onions, chopped fine
- ½ cup ground, blanched almonds
- 1 tsp. cardamon
- ½ tsp. red pepper flakes
- ½ tsp. cloves
- 1½ tsp. salt
- 1 tsp. pepper
- 1 piece of fresh ginger the size of a quarter, minced
- 4 tbsp. melted butter
- 2 tbsp. water

1. Take the skin off the breasts and prick the chicken all over with a fork so that it will absorb the spices.
2. Mix remaining ingredients to make a smooth paste.
3. Spread paste all over the chicken.
4. Place in a buttered baking dish making sure that the pieces don't overlap.
4. Roast in a 350 degree oven, covered, for 1 hour.
5. Remove cover and roast 20 minutes more.

When we drove through the Swiss Alps, the first region we entered in Italy was the Piedmont region and this was our first meal there or, at least, this is how I tried to copy it. It's especially nice for dinner parties because it can be prepared in advance and just stuck under the broiler at the last moment.

piedmont chicken *

4 boneless chicken breasts
¾ cup flour
salt and pepper
4 tbsp. butter
1 bouillon cube
¾ cup hot water
¼ cup white wine
1 cup grated parmesan cheese
3 tbsp. fresh parsley, chopped

1. Pound chicken breasts until quite flat and cut in half.
2. Mix flour, salt and pepper and coat chicken lightly.
3. Heat butter in frying pan and brown chicken pieces.
4. Turn heat to medium and cook chicken until done, turning every so often.
5. Set chicken aside and keep warm.
5. Dissolve bouillon in hot water.
6. Place bouillon and wine in the same skillet and cook until liquid is reduced by half.
7. Place chicken in a roasting dish, pour liquid over it and sprinkle with parmesan cheese.
8. Place under broiler and broil until cheese is melted.

An exotic dish, this one is a little too rich for my blood, so I try not to overdo it. It's best made with cream, but you can always try half-and-half and serve it a little more often. It comes from Thailand and is quite delicious. Save the coconut for the coconut cake in my dessert section.

coconut chicken *

2 cups heavy cream
1½ cups dried, grated coconut
6 chicken breasts
4 cloves garlic, minced
½ tsp. dried red pepper flakes
1 small onion, minced
1 tbsp. grated lemon rind
1 tsp. coriander
1 tbsp. soy sauce
3 tbsp. ground peanuts

1. Put cream and coconut in a saucepan; place over low heat and bring to a boil, then remove from fire and let sit for 30 minutes.
2. Drain and save coconut for another use.
3. Place chicken and coconut milk in a heavy saucepan; cover and cook for 40 minutes over low heat, turning chicken occasionally.
4. Add remaining ingredients and cook for another 15 minutes, again turning chicken to coat with sauce.
5. Serve with rice.

Most people I know hardly ever use a popular Greek pasta called orzo. Fortunately, we knew a fine Greek cook and friend named Bessie Ahouris from Silver Spring, Md., who fed us this. Look for orzo in the pasta section. It actually looks a bit like rice.

bessie's chicken and orzo **

2 small chickens, cut in small pieces
salt and pepper
2 tbsp. butter
1 16-oz. can tomatoes, drained
½ tsp. garlic powder
2 cups orzo
½ to 1 cup water

1. Place chickens in a roasting pan, sprinkle with salt and pepper and dot with butter.
2. Bake in a 350 degree oven until nicely browned (about 1 to 1½ hours).
3. Remove chicken and set aside.
4. Place tomatoes sprinkled with garlic powder in the roasting pan and brown in oven. As tomatoes start to brown on the edges, keep scraping the sides of the pan and cook for around 20 minutes.
5. In the meantime, cook orzo according to directions on box and drain.
6. When tomatoes are brown, return chicken to pan; add orzo and enough water to make a good consistency.
7. Place pan in oven and cook an additional 10 minutes to blend all flavors.
8. Check for seasonings and serve.

An experiment — slightly different with a nice spiciness!

chicken piquant *

- 1 oz. dried Italian mushrooms
- 2 cups canned tomatoes
- 3 tbsp. oil
- 2 tbsp. paprika
- 1 chicken, cut into frying pieces
- 1 cup hard salami, cut in thin 3 inch strips
- 2 cloves garlic, chopped
- ½ cup dry white wine
- 1 cup sliced fresh mushrooms
- 1 tsp. red pepper flakes
- salt and pepper

1. Put dry mushrooms in a bowl; cover with warm water and let sit one hour.
2. Put tomatoes in a saucepan and simmer until they are reduced by about half.
3. Heat oil in heavy skillet, sprinkle chicken with paprika, and brown well on both sides.
4. Add salami and garlic and cook for 3 minutes.
5. Pour off fat, add wine and reduced tomato sauce to skillet.
6. Drain and squeeze moisture out of soaked Italian mushrooms.
7. Add the Italian mushrooms, fresh mushrooms, red pepper flakes, salt, and pepper and cover.
8. Cook over low heat for about one hour until chicken is done.

When I was in college, I had a Greek boyfriend who used to take me home for Sunday dinners. I was fascinated with his Greek family, their friends, their rituals, and especially their cooking. At my own home, Sunday chicken dinner usually meant a roast chicken with mashed potatoes. At my girlfriend's home, stewed chicken with boiled potatoes was the order of the day. This Greek lady did it differently and I've tried to approximate it here. I believe she cooked everything in the pan from the beginning, but I find it easier to parboil the vegetables first, so that everything gets done on time. If you find there is too little juice to baste with, add a little more wine.

sunday greek dinner **

1 frying chicken, washed, patted dry, and cut in pieces
2 tbsp. oil
juice from 1 large lemon
1 large clove garlic, minced
⅓ cup oregano
salt and pepper
¾ to 1 cup white wine
4 potatoes, peeled and halved
4 large carrots, cut in strips
8 small onions, peeled

1. Lay the chicken in a large flat baking pan.
2. With a pastry brush, dab the oil on the chicken pieces to coat them.
3. Pour the lemon juice over the chicken.
4. Place the garlic on top of the chicken pieces and then sprinkle generously with the oregano, saving some of it for the vegetables.
5. Add salt and pepper and pour the wine into the bottom of the pan.
6. Cover with foil and place in a 350 degree oven.
7. Cook the chicken for 45 minutes.
8. Parboil the potatoes and carrots in boiling water for 10 minutes and then add the onions for 10 minutes more. Drain. (Save cooking water for soup.)
9. When the chicken has cooked for 45 minutes, place the parboiled vegetables in the pan and sprinkle with the rest of the oregano, salt and pepper. Cover and bake 15 minutes more.
10. Remove foil and bake for the last 15 minutes, basting with the pan juices.

Valdi Sherwood is a very attractive woman who possesses boundless optimism and deals with assorted children, animals, jobs and traveling with great cheerfulness and equanimity. She and her mate, Cliff Irving, are friends whose company we have enjoyed for a number of years. Valdi laughs easily and I am always impressed with her resourcefulness and zest for life. When you prepare her dish, make sure you choose a rice pilaf that has pure ingredients.

valdi's chicken pilaf **

1 9 oz. package of rice pilaf
½ cup raisins
½ cup slivered almonds
1 8½ oz. can artichoke hearts, drained
2 tbsp. safflower oil
1 medium onion, chopped
2 cloves garlic, sliced
2 chicken breasts, skinned and cut into thin strips
1 cup white wine
1 tsp. dry mustard
salt and pepper
½ cup sour cream

1. Prepare a package of rice pilaf according to directions.
2. When done, add ½ cup raisins, ½ cup slivered almonds, the artichoke hearts, and stir well.
3. Heat oil in a large frying pan, and saute onions and garlic until golden.
4. Add chicken and stir fry over high heat until chicken has lost its pink color.
5. Add white wine, and stir for a few minutes in order to deglaze pan, scraping often.
6. Add mustard, salt, pepper, and sour cream and heat through.
7. Reheat pilaf.
8. Pour chicken over pilaf and serve immediately.

One of the easiest of chicken curry recipes, this doesn't take days to prepare. You can serve it with rice and all the standard condiments, like coconut, chutney, chopped hard-boiled eggwhites, mashed hard-boiled egg yolks, and peanuts.

easy chicken curry **

1 whole chicken (4 to 5 pounds)
2 quarts water
3 tbsp. peanut oil
3 tbsp. curry powder
1 clove garlic, minced
1 cup onion, diced
2 apples, peeled and diced
1 tomato, chopped
1 banana, sliced
dash of cayenne pepper
1 bay leaf
salt and pepper
2 cups chicken broth

1. Put chicken into 2 quarts water and simmer until done. Save broth.
2. Skin and bone chicken and shred chicken finely.
3. Saute curry powder in oil for a few minutes.
4. Add garlic and onions and cook a few minutes more.
5. Add the shredded chicken and stir to coat well.
6. Add apples, tomatoes, bananas, cayenne pepper, bay leaf, salt and pepper.
7. Cook 1 minute.
8. Add 2 cups of the chicken broth, cover and simmer 20 minutes.
9. Remove cover and cook 15 minutes more.

Baked chicken salad is a marvelous party recipe from Dorothy and Wilson Stone, our neighbors in East Hampton. I always enjoy their Sunday lunches held in their sun-filled dining room — flowers on the tables, music softly playing in the background, interesting guests, many laughs. They entertain with great style and are warm, gracious hosts. Dorothy prepared this for us on one such Sunday, but said that it was actually given to her by Wilson's Mother. It's such a convenient dish because it can be made way ahead and just popped into the oven when guests arrive.

baked chicken salad ***

4 cups cooked, salted chicken, cubed
2 cups celery, diced
¾ cup slivered almonds
1 8-oz. can water chestnuts, sliced
¾ cup cheddar cheese, grated
1½ cups mayonnaise, preferably homemade
½ can cream of mushroom soup
3 tbsp. lemon juice
6 slices thin white bread
½ stick butter

1. Mix all ingredients except bread and butter and place in a flat baking dish.
2. Trim crusts from bread and cut in cubes.
3. Melt butter in skillet and saute bread cubes until brown and crunchy.
4. Sprinkle cubes over chicken and bake in a 350 degree oven for 45 minutes.

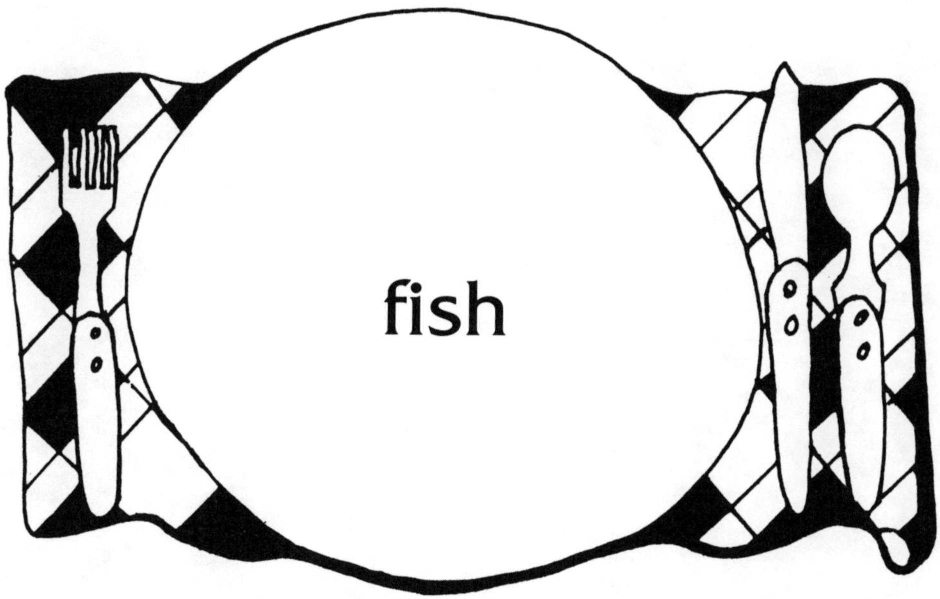
fish

A recipe from Cambodia, this is called michha trong kroeung. It is quite easy to prepare and although I like a rather delicate white fleshed fish, I imagine you could use a heavier kind like codfish or monkfish for both economy or variety, making sure to cook the fish longer before adding the sauce.

cambodian fish with scallion sauce **

5 tbsp. peanut oil
1½ lbs. fish fillets
4 cloves garlic, sliced
12 scallions, halved and sliced into 3 inch pieces
1 tbsp. paprika
2 tsp. fennel or anise seeds
1 tbsp. lemon juice
dash of salt and pepper
½ cup water
½ cup chopped parsley

1. Heat oil in large skillet and add fish.
2. Cook just a few moments until fish is almost done, turning once.
3. Remove fish to baking dish and set aside.
4. Add remaining ingredients to skillet, except parsley, and simmer over low flame for 15 minutes, adding a little more water if necessary.
5. Place fish in baking dish, spoon sauce over it and bake in 350 degree oven for 15 minutes.
6. Sprinkle with fresh parsley and serve.

This particular recipe coming from my step-mother is unusual. She used sour cream, but I use half yogurt and half sour cream. You can use all yogurt or all sour cream.

fern's chinese tuna *

2 tbsp. peanut oil
½ cup onion, minced
½ cup green pepper, minced
1 10 oz. can tuna, well drained
½ can tomato paste
2 cups water
¼ tsp. black pepper
¼ tsp. red pepper flakes
½ pint yogurt
½ pint sour cream
4 cups Chinese noodles

1. Heat oil in frying pan and add onions and green peppers.
2. Cook until onions become transparent.
3. Add tuna and mix well with a fork.
4. Stir tomato paste in water and mix well.
5. Add tomato paste mixture to tuna along with both black and red pepper and stir.
6. Lower heat and simmer for 15 minutes.
7. Just before serving, stir in the yogurt and sour cream.
8. Pour over warmed Chinese noodles.

A lovely and different way to prepare shrimp, this is a good party dinner if you're not having too many people since shrimp is rather expensive. It can be made early in the day and reheated before dinner. It's a very old recipe of mine and comes from Ceylon.

ceylon shrimp curry **

1 lb. shrimp, shelled and deveined
1 medium onion, sliced in rings
1 tsp. red pepper
⅛ tsp. tumeric
2 cloves garlic, sliced
2 slices fresh ginger or ½ tsp. dry ginger
1 tsp. salt
2 inch piece cinnamon stick
¾ cup milk
1 tbsp. oil
juice of ½ lime
1 tsp. cornstarch
¼ cup water

1. Place shrimp, ½ of the onion, red pepper, tumeric, garlic, ginger, salt, cinnamon stick and milk in a saucepan and boil gently for 10 minutes, stirring occasionally.
2. Brown the rest of the onions in the oil.
3. Add onions and lime juice to shrimp and simmer 10 more minutes.
4. Mix cornstarch with water, add to shrimp and cook until slightly thickened.
5. Serve with boiled rice.

Judy Wolfe came over one morning and said, "I had the best fish dish last night. You'll have to try it." So, the next night I tried it out on my husband and mother-in-law. They both felt it was an interesting and unusual dish, so I'm passing it along like a chain letter.

judy's fish with mushrooms *

4 fish fillets (bluefish, flounder, fluke etc.)
¼ cup mayonnaise
4 tbsp. yogurt
2 tbsp. Dijon mustard
2 tbsp. lemon juice
salt and pepper
1 large onion, sliced
½ lb. mushrooms, sliced
2 tbsp. butter

1. Place fish fillets in a flat baking dish.
2. Mix mayonnaise, yogurt, mustard, lemon juice, salt, and pepper.
3. Spread sauce over fish and bake in a 350 degree oven until fish flakes easily.
4. In the meantime, saute onions and mushrooms in butter until soft.
5. When fish is done, pour the mushroom and onion sauce over the fish; place the fish under the broiler for a few minutes and serve.

My good friend Florence Grey invented this dish, invited us to dinner to sample it, and then donated it to my cookbook. Now, that's a true friend. I found that the directions on preparing couscous differ on each brand, so you need to follow the directions on your particular box. Florence uses "Harissa," a hot sauce found in gourmet shops, but you can use another brand or simply cayenne or red pepper flakes.

florence grey's scallops with couscous **

1 1-lb. box couscous
½ tbsp. "Harissa" or comparable hot sauce
3 tbsp. butter
1 clove garlic crushed
1 lb. scallops
2 tbsp. parsley, minced

1. Cook couscous according to directions.
2. Mix it well with the hot sauce. You may want to add more or less sauce depending on how hot you like your food.
3. Keep the couscous warm while you cook the scallops.
4. Heat butter with the garlic and saute scallops very quickly for just a few minutes until they turn from pink to white. Do not overcook.
5. Pour scallops into couscous, scraping the pan and mix well.
6. Garnish with parsley and serve immediately.

I have never really been able to make sole amandine that pleases me. One evening our good friends Bernice and Morton Hunt treated us to dinner at their favorite restaurant in the Hamptons. Everyone ordered sole amandine and it was truly superb. "Bernice," I said, "what do you think is the secret of this dish"? Bernice is such a superior cook that I thought if anyone knew, she would. "I think they dip it lightly in flour and then cook it quickly over a very high heat in lots of butter," she replied. The next day, I went and bought sole fillets and proceeded to make sole amandine for dinner. Bernice was right. Incidentally, you can use any thin white fillet of fish; flounder is a good choice but it must be very fresh.

sole amandine *

4 fillets of sole
½ cup flour
⅓ cup butter
⅓ cup slivered almonds
lemon wedges
parsley

1. Lightly flour the fish fillets on both sides.
2. Heat butter over high flame in a heavy frying pan and saute fillets in butter until done. This should take only a few moments and the fish should be turned once.
3. Put fish on a platter, lower heat, quickly saute the almonds lightly and pour almonds and butter over the fish.
4. Serve with lemon wedges and parsley.

A nice way to prepare a cheaper kind of fish, this is a simple and tasty fish stew. You can use a thick filleted fish like anglerfish, monkfish, or I suppose cod. Serve with crusty french bread to dip into the sauce.

good cheap fish *

3 tbsp. olive oil
4 fish fillets
2 tbsp. safflower oil
1 large onion, minced
1 scallion, cut in pieces
3 tomatoes, skinned and quartered
¾ cup white wine
salt and pepper
1 tsp. basil
a sprinkling of red pepper flakes
2 tbsp. minced parsley

1. Heat olive oil in frying pan, add fish and fry for 5 minutes, turning once. Set aside.
2. In a large pan, saute onions and scallions in safflower oil for a few minutes.
3. Add remaining ingredients and bring to a boil.
4. Turn heat low and simmer for about 20 minutes, so that the sauce cooks down and is not watery.
5. Add the fish to the sauce and cook over low heat until fish is done and it flakes easily.

I had never used a Chinese spice called star anise, so when I found an old recipe in my files calling for it, I decided to try it. It's a very pretty spice and indeed looks like a star. It imparts a very delicate flavor to this dish.

chinese flounder **

¼ cup safflower oil
1 lb. flounder fillets or any kind of delicate white fish.
1 clove garlic, minced
1 tsp. ginger, minced
2 scallions, cut in 1-inch lengths
½ cup sliced mushrooms
1 tsp. salt
4 tsp. tamari
2 tsp. dry sherry
1 cup chicken stock
1 clove star anise

1. Heat oil in a large pan and saute the fillets for ½ minute on each side.
2. Add garlic, ginger, scallions, mushrooms, salt, tamari, and sherry and cook 1 minute.
3. Slowly add the chicken stock.
4. Turn heat on high and add the star anise.
5. When the stock begins to boil, turn the heat to low, cover and cook 5 to 10 minutes or until the fish is done.

A concoction that came about when I wanted to use some leftovers and I didn't have enough for a meal. Kasha Imperial was created by adding sausage and a few other ingredients. It's reminiscent of a paella and of course you can substitute different kinds of fish, including mussels, lobster etc.

kasha imperial **

- 3 cloves garlic, mashed
- 2 onions, sliced in rings
- 1 green pepper, seeded and cut in thin strips
- ¼ cup olive oil
- 2 tbsp. curry powder
- 3 lbs. fish, such as weakfish, blackfish etc.
- 2 lbs. Italian hot sausage
- 1 cup dry white wine
- 2 bay leaves
- 1 2-lb. can Italian plum tomatoes
- 4 cups cooked kasha
- 1 dozen small clams
- ½ lb. scallops
- 1 fresh red tomato, cut in cubes

1. Saute garlic, onions, and green pepper in olive oil until the onion is golden.
2. Add curry powder and cook 2 minutes.
3. Push vegetables aside, add fish and brown lightly.
4. Remove fish from pan and set aside.
5. Add sausages and brown well on all sides, pricking to release any grease.
6. Remove grease from pan and add wine, bay leaves, canned tomatoes and simmer gently until slightly reduced. To this point, everything can be made well in advance.
7. Return fish to pan along with the cooked kasha and simmer until both fish and sausage is done.
8. Add clams and scallops; cover and cook until clams have opened.
9. Place in large serving bowl and garnish with freshly chopped tomatoes.

Florence Grey made this tangy fish dish for us one evening with the help of her husband Jerry, who sliced all the scallions beautifully like a fine oriental chef. He made such delicate slivers of scallions that the dish was very pretty to look at as well as tasting very, very good. While she broiled bluefish fillets, you can substitute other kinds of fish and it can be steamed instead of baked. The secret is the sauce. Make sure most of the liquid boils away, so it isn't runny when you pile it on the fish.

florence's tangy fish *

- 2 tbsp. butter
- 2 bunches of scallion tops, slivered very thin and cut in 3 inch pieces
- 1 piece of fresh ginger, about the size of a quarter and sliced in small thin pieces
- ½ tsp. Chinese hot chili paste (found in oriental stores)
- ⅓ cup white wine
- 4 bluefish fillets
- 2 tbsp. olive oil

1. Melt butter in skillet, add scallion tops and ginger and saute for a few minutes.
2. Add the Chinese chili and wine; stir and simmer over low heat for about 10 to 15 minutes until the sauce has cooked down.
3. In the meantime, brush the fillets with olive oil and broil until done.
4. Spoon some of the hot sauce on top of each fillet and serve immediately.

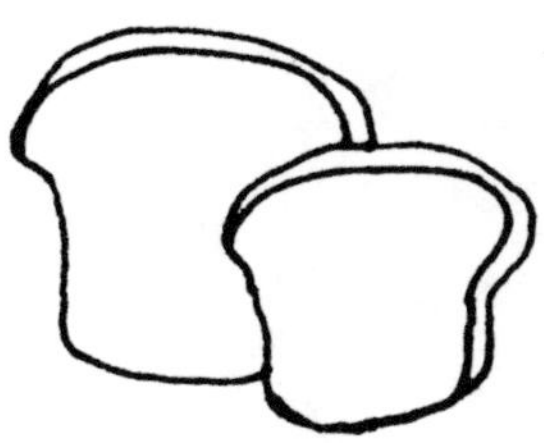

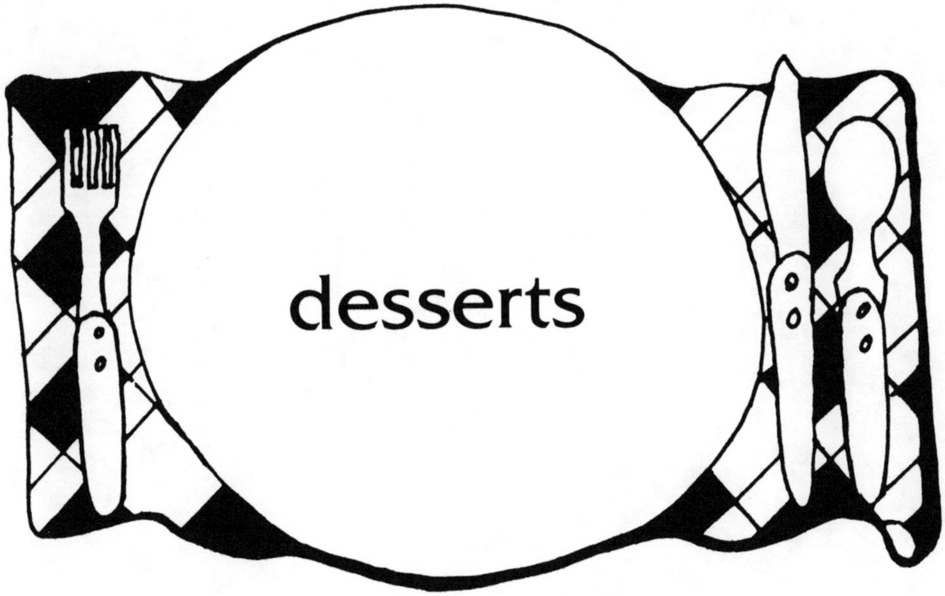
desserts

This is a delicious dessert that came from my former mother-in-law. It can be served plain or with fresh fruit.

russian cream *

- 1 cup cream
- ¾ cup sugar
- 2 tsp. gelatin
- 1 cup cold water
- 1 cup sour cream
- ¼ tsp. salt
- ½ tsp. vanilla

1. Heat cream and sugar in top of double boiler until luke warm.
2. Soak gelatin in 1 cup cold water for 5 minutes and then add to cream.
3. Stir very well until dissolved and then place in refrigerator to chill.
4. When mixture begins to thicken, add sour cream, salt and vanilla.
5. Stir well and put into mold or individual dishes to set.

A very simple dessert, easy to prepare and not very fattening, this comes from Pam Topham.

applesauce fluff*

- 5 eggwhites, whipped into peaks
- 1 quart applesauce
- sprinkling of fresh nutmeg

1. Fold eggwhites gently into applesauce.
2. Sprinkle with nutmeg and serve.

When Marty was interviewing people for a biography of the psychiatrist, Fritz Perls, one of Dr. Perl's relatives served us this rich and wonderful dessert during a coffee break.

bavarian apple slice ***

1½ cups flour
½ tsp. salt
3 tbsp. sugar
½ cup butter
1 egg yolk
5 tbsp. milk
1 to 1½ lbs. tart apples, peeled and sliced
2 tbsp. seedless raisins
2 tbsp. golden raisins
3 tbsp. fresh bread crumbs
1 tbsp. brown sugar
1 tsp. cinnamon
whipped cream or sour cream as a side dish if desired.

1. Sift flour, salt and sugar into a mixing bowl.
2. Cut butter into mixture with a pastry fork or knives.
3. Mix egg yolk with milk and stir into pastry to bind together. (You may have to add more milk.)
4. Chill 30 minutes.
5. Mix apples, both kinds of raisins, bread crumbs, brown sugar and cinnamon.
6. Knead pastry lightly on a floured board.
7. Divide into two parts — a ⅔ piece, and a ⅓ piece.
8. Roll out the larger piece so that it will fit an 8-inch pie tin.
9. Place it gently in the tin and fill with the fruit.
10. Roll out the smaller piece and cut into ¼-inch strips.
11. Cover the pie with the strips to make a lattice work, using a little milk or water to seal the edges.
12. Bake in a 375 degree over for about 35 minutes.
13. Serve with whipped or sour cream.

A wonderful dessert from Indiana again, pecan surprise squares are easy to prepare and take very little time.

pecan surprise squares *

1 egg, beaten
1 tsp. vanilla
1 cup brown sugar, firmly packed
½ cup flour
¼ tsp. salt
¼ tsp. baking soda
1 cup pecans, coarsely chopped

1. Stir egg, vanilla, and brown sugar together.
2. Sift flour, salt and baking soda.
3. Add to brown sugar and stir well.
4. Stir in pecans.
5. Spread in a buttered square dish. Use your fingers to press mixture down, but do not worry if it doesn't completely cover, as it will spread in the baking.
6. Bake at 350 degrees for 18 to 20 minutes. Mixture will be soft when you take it from the oven.
7. Let it cool slightly and then cut in squares.

A dish I concocted, pears with ginger can be served with sour cream instead of yogurt — not as healthy and slimming, but very nice.

pears with ginger *

4 fresh pears, peeled and cut in quarters
1 cup water
¼ cup raw sugar
1 cup yogurt
¼ cup honey
2 tsp. crystallized ginger, cut in small pieces

1. Stir pears in water and sugar over low heat until done.
2. Combine yogurt and honey and mix well.
3. Divide pears and a little bit of the syrup into four dessert dishes.
4. Spoon yogurt mixture on top and sprinkle each with the ginger.

What an elegant dessert! We were having friends over for a communal meal and evening of music when Christina showed up with a dish that had everyone ooing and aahing. She said that no barbecue was complete in her native Australia without a "Pavlova." She graciously gave me the recipe and I tried it out the next night for my husband and two friends. It was consumed in a moment with great relish and gusto. You can substitute any kinds of fruit.

pavlova **

- 4 egg whites
- pinch of salt
- pinch of cream of tartar
- ½ cup sugar
- ½ tsp. vanilla
- ½ cup slivered almonds or walnut bits.
- ½ pint whipping cream
- 2 tbsp. brown sugar
- 1 large pear, peeled and sliced
- 1 banana, sliced
- 1½ cups strawberries, sliced

1. Place eggwhites, salt, and cream of tartar in a bowl and beat until eggwhites are stiff.
2. Slowly beat in sugar.
3. Add vanilla and fold in nuts.
4. Place meringue on a large piece of buttered foil and fold up edges of foil slightly to contain meringue.
5. Bake in a 200 degree oven for one hour.
6. Allow it to cool in the oven, so the meringue won't crack.
7. Whip cream into peaks.
8. Fold in sugar and fruit.
9. Spread whipped cream and fruit on meringue and cut in pie-shaped wedges.

orange delight *

- 4 oranges, skinned and cut into bite sized pieces
- ½ cup triple sec liquor
- ½ cup marmalade
- ½ cup almonds, blanched and slivered

1. Marinate orange pieces in triple sec for 3 hours.
2. Pour off liquid and combine it with marmalade.
3. Mix the marmalade and triple sec in a blender for a few minutes.
4. In 4 individual dessert bowls, layer the orange pieces with the almonds.
5. Pour the sauce over each dessert and chill before serving.

Esalen grows many of its own fruits and berries and this dessert was a fine way to end one of their marvelous meals. I am going to list the fruits that they used, but you can adapt it to whatever you see at your market that looks fresh and delectable. I like to serve the dressing on the side because the fruit looks so pretty, but of course you can mix it beforehand.

esalen fruit ambrosia **

1 big chunk of watermelon, seeded and cut in bite-sized chunks
1 bunch of grapes, seeded and separated
2 apples, skinned and cut in slices
4 nectarines or peaches, sliced
3 bananas, peeled and sliced
a handful of either sunflower seeds or slivered almonds

1. Place all the fruit in a bowl and serve with the topping on the side.

Ambrosia Topping

¾ lb. of whipped cream cheese at room temperature
½ cup yogurt
⅓ cup honey
¼ tsp. cinnamon
dash of powdered cloves

1. Mix cream cheese and yogurt well.
2. Add honey, cinnamon and cloves and blend into cream cheese mixture.

This is a traditional recipe out in Indiana and made superbly by Grandma Reiber. No Christmas was complete without it. I thought that I had never eaten suet before and it was strange to think of putting it into a dessert until I remembered how mince pie was made.

grandma reiber's suet pudding **

½ cup suet, ground
½ cup molasses
½ cup milk
1½ cups flour
½ tsp. baking powder
½ tsp. nutmeg
½ tsp. cinnamon
½ tsp. baking soda
1 cup raisins

1. Mix suet, molasses and milk.
2. Sift all dry ingredients and add to suet mixture.
3. Fold in raisins.
4. Place in a pudding mold with a cover and boil in rapidly boiling water until done — 1½ to 2 hours. If necessary, add more boiling water.

Note: If you don't have a pudding mold, I have heard that you can put the dough in a wet towel, tie it securely and then boil as usual in a pan of water.

pam topham's wonderful chestnut mousse **

7 egg whites
pinch of cream of tartar
½ cup sugar
1 cup chestnut (marron) puree
3 tbsp. cream
1 tbsp. vanilla
6 egg yolks
1 heavy cream
nutmeg

1. Whip egg whites, cream of tartar, and ¼ cup of the sugar to form soft peaks.
2. In a double boiler, stir the other ¼ cup of the sugar, chestnut puree, the 3 tbsp. cream and vanilla until smooth.
3. Whip the pint of cream into peaks.
4. Mix the whipped egg whites, the chestnut puree sauce and the whipped cream gently together and sprinkle with nutmeg.
5. Chill 8 hours before serving.

My mother-in-law Marcia always brings goodies when she comes to visit. This is one of them and I think that it's one of the best recipes for carrot cake that I have tasted.

marcia's carrot cake **

1 cup flour
¾ cup sugar
1 tsp. salt
1 tsp. baking soda
1 tsp. cinnamon
2 eggs, beaten
½ cup corn oil
1 tbsp. lemon juice
1½ cups carrots, grated
½ cup walnuts, chopped
½ cup raisins
1 tsp. grated lemon peel

1. Sift dry ingredients into a large bowl.
2. Add beaten eggs and oil.
3. Stir in lemon juice.
4. Add carrots, nuts, raisins, grated lemon peel, and mix thoroughly.
5. Pour into a greased loaf pan and bake at 350 degrees about 50 to 60 minutes until done.

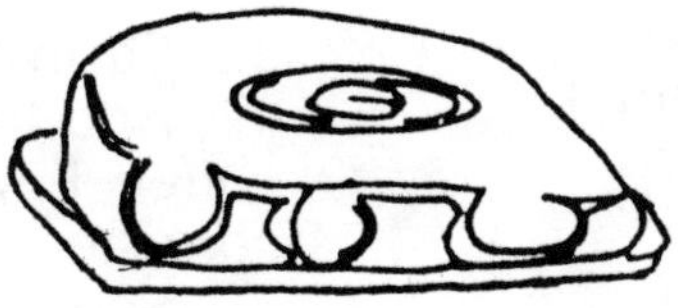

From a neighbor Shirley to Aunt Florrie to my mother-in-law, that's how this noodle pudding came to me. I try to use cornflakes from the health food store and low fat cream cheese.

noodle pudding **

6 eggs
1 pt. sour cream
1 cup sugar (reserve 2 tbsp. for topping)
½ lb. melted butter (reserve 2 tbsp. for topping)
12 oz. package of cream cheese, softened
1 lb. flat noodles, cooked
2 cups cornflakes, crushed

1. Beat eggs with sour cream.
2. Add butter and sugar.
3. Add cream cheese and noodles and mix well.
4. Place in a 9 x 13 greased baking dish.
5. Mix the cornflakes with the reserved melted butter and sugar.
6. Sprinkle on top and put in refrigerator overnight.
7. Bake at 325 degrees for 1 hour.

A dessert not to have too often for obvious reasons, I like this cake of my mother-in-law's because though it's not sickeningly sweet, it certainly satisfies all sweet tooths. She started making this in the 1930's, incidentally, so it's a 50 year old recipe.

marcia's chocolate creole cake ***

½ cup shortening
1½ cups brown sugar, well packed
3 eggs, separated
1 tsp. baking powder, sifted
2 cups flour, sifted
1 tsp. baking soda dissolved in 1 tsp. boiling water
1 cup warm milk
2 squares unsweetened Baker's chocolate, shaved.

1. Cream shortening and sugar.
2. Add egg yolks and stir.
3. Add the baking powder and flour alternately with milk.
4. Add dissolved baking soda.
5. Add chocolate and mix well.
6. Beat egg whites until stiff and fold in cake mixture.
7. Bake in a greased tube pan at 350 degrees for 40 to 45 minutes.

Mocha Creamy Frosting

1 3-oz. package cream cheese
¾ cup confectionary sugar, sifted
1 tsp. vanilla
1 square melted chocolate
2 tbsp. strong coffee

1. Blend cream cheese with sugar.
2. Add vanilla.
3. Stir in melted chocolate and mix well.
4. Add the coffee and stir, using more coffee if you need a better spreading consistency.
5. Spread over the tops and sides of the cooled cake.

The most beautiful island in the Carribean, my husband and I agree, is Dominica, not to be confused with the Dominican Republican. It's a shangri la, showering intermittently throughout the day with profusions of rainbows, beaches of black sand, mountain peaks ringed with clouds and very few tourists. This is a dessert from Dominica, rich, but special.

dominican custard pudding *

3½ cups milk
6 tbsp. butter
1½ cups brown sugar
4 tbsp. cornstarch
2 eggs
½ tsp. vanilla

1. Scald milk in a pan with the butter.
2. Mix with remaining ingredients; stir well and pour into a buttered baking dish.
3. Place dish in a pan of water and bake at 325 degrees for about an hour or until an inserted knife comes out clean.
4. Cool and serve.

This recipe was given to me about 25 years ago out in Clinton, Indiana, by a friend named Mary Alice Osmon. It was interesting because it used mayonnaise. Whoever heard of that! Surprisingly, my husband, who doesn't like chocolate cake, loved this because he felt that it wasn't "dry" like other cakes. Here it is.

mary alice osmon's chocolate mayonnaise cake **

1 cup flour
¾ cup sugar
¼ cup cocoa
1 tsp. baking soda
½ cup warm water
½ cup mayonnaise

1. Mix all the dry ingredients.
2. Add warm water and mix.
3. Add mayonnaise and mix well.
4. Pour into a lightly oiled flat baking pan about 9″ by 13″ in size and bake in a 350 degree oven about 30 to 35 minutes until done.

Frosting for Mayonnaise Cake

½ box sifted powdered sugar
¼ cup cocoa
½ stick butter, softened
¼ cup karo syrup
1 tbsp. milk or cream
1 tsp. vanilla

1. Mix powdered sugar and cocoa making sure that all lumps are dissolved.
2. Add butter and cream well.
3. Add syrup, cream or milk and vanilla and mix until smooth.
4. Spread on cooled cake.

My grandmother made only three different kinds of cookies — peanut butter, chocolate chip and oatmeal — but she never failed to make one large batch of them every Saturday morning. This is her recipe for peanut butter cookies.

old fashioned peanut butter cookies **

2½ cups sifted all purpose flour
1 tsp. baking powder
1½ tsp. baking soda
½ tsp. salt
½ cup butter (1 stick)
½ cup Crisco
1 cup sugar
1 cup brown sugar, lightly packed
2 eggs, beaten
1 tsp. vanilla
1½ cups peanut butter

1. Sift flour, baking powder, soda and salt.
2. In another bowl, cream butter, Crisco and sugars until smooth.
3. Add eggs and vanilla.
4. Add peanut butter and stir until it is well mixed.
5. Gradually add dry ingredients.
6. Divide dough in two balls, wrap in wax paper and chill for several hours or overnight.
7. When ready to bake, roll small amounts of dough between your palms to make little balls.
8. Place balls on cookie sheet and flatten with a fork to make ridges.
9. Bake at 350 degrees for 8 to 10 minutes.

This is a delicious coconut cake, very different from your usual kind. Since I like to make coconut milk for some Thai and Cambodian dishes, this gives me a use for the left-over coconut.

coconut cake **

1 stick butter
1 cup sugar
4 egg yolks
¾ cup farina, sifted
½ cup flour, sifted
1 tsp. baking powder, sifted
1½ cups grated coconut
1 tsp. vanilla
4 egg whites, stiffly beaten

1. Cream butter and sugar.
2. Stir in egg yolks.
3. Add dry ingredients and mix well.
4. Add grated coconut and vanilla.
5. Fold in egg whites.
6. Pour into lightly buttered or greased square pan and bake for 30 to 40 minutes or until a toothpick comes out clean.

It seems that whenever I want strawberry shortcake, I can only find those tasteless, preservative laden cakes displayed so prominently in the stores during strawberry season. The only alternative is to use Bisquick and make your own. The problem is that Bisquick has preservatives also. My Mother solved this dilemma for me by sending me a recipe from her childhood. This is what shortcake should taste like. Of course, you can smother it with any fruit in season before topping it with heavy cream or whipped cream.

You can also simplify this by just pressing dough into a flat baking dish and cutting it in wedges.

mrs. biffar's shortcake **

2 cups flour
4 tsp. baking powder
½ tsp. salt
1 tbsp. sugar
¼ cup shortening
1 egg, well beaten
⅔ cup milk

1. Sift dry ingredients.
2. Cut in shortening until mixture has the consistency of coarse crumbs.
3. Add egg and milk and stir just to mix.
4. Put dough on a floured board and pat it down so that it's about ⅓ inch thick.
5. With a round cookie cutter, cut out rounds for the shortcake.
6. Place rounds on cookie sheet and bake in a 425 degree oven for 20 minutes.

Whenever Ron Millican comes to dinner or we dine at his house, we have one of a variety of lovely fruit pies made by him. Ron is a nice looking, articulate man who recently married a vivacious young actress named Laurie Heineman. They are both fun to spend time with. The other night Ron mentioned how easy this dessert was to prepare and I thought it would be a good addition to this book. It can be served with yogurt, whipped cream or ice cream, if you wish.

ron's fruit pie *

1 unbaked pieshell
2 cups fresh fruit in season (like apples, peaches, pears or berries) or a combination of fruits, peeled and sliced
¼ to½ cup pure maple syrup

1. Bake pie shell in a 400° oven until slightly browned.
2. Arrange fruit slices in a nice pattern in the pie shell.
3. Drizzle maple syrup over fruit.
4. Bake in a 350 degree oven for 15 minutes or until fruit is done.

A holiday topping from Jane Wilson's Party Box, it's easy to see why this is one of New York City's best catering services. Serve this over vanilla ice cream.

jane's cranberry jubilee *

2 cups raw cranberries
¾ cup water
12 oz. red currant jelly
¼ cup raw sugar
½ cup rum
¼ cup brandy
grated rind of 1 orange

1. Cook cranberries in water until they pop.
2. Add the rest of the ingredients and simmer for 10 minutes.
3. Cool and store in refrigerator until ready to use.

Judy Wolfe exclaimed one day, "If you're writing a cookbook, you must include the mousse that my friend Judy Long makes. It's so delicious and doesn't take any time at all. You just put everything in a blender." However, I must caution you to use only the regular chocolate chips. The first time I tried it, my husband picked up milk chocolate chips and the mousse wouldn't jell.

judy long's chocolate mousse *

1 6-oz. package of semi-sweet chocolate chips
2 eggs
2 tbsp. triple sec or rum
3 tbsp. hot strong coffee
¾ cup milk, scalded not boiled

1. Put all these ingredients in a blender and whip at high speed for two minutes.
2. Pour into individual dishes and chill until set. This takes a couple of hours. Easy!

My Mother gave this recipe of my Grandmother Honey's to me when I was starting to write this book. When I tried it out, I felt a very warm and satisfying feeling to know that I was cooking one of my grandmother's recipes. I liked the continuity and a few days later passed the recipe along to my daughter, Liza. Now, there is a third generation preparing it. Incidentally, this turned out to be my favorite cupcake recipe, much better than your ordinary yellow cupcakes with chocolate or vanilla frosting.

honey's "quilting bees" *

2 cups raisins
2 cups water
1½ cups sugar
½ cup shortening
2 eggs
2½ cups flour
2 tsp. cinnamon
½ tsp. cloves
1 tsp. nutmeg
¼ tsp. salt
2 tsp. baking powder
1 cup walnut pieces

1. Boil raisins in water for 10 minutes and drain.
2. Cream sugar and shortening.
3. Add eggs and stir.
4. Add all dry ingredients and mix well.
5. Stir in nuts and raisins.
6. Put in a lightly greased muffin tin and bake in a 350 degree oven until done (30 to 40 minutes, depending on the size muffin tins you are using).

breads

mrs. corner's lemon-sesame bread *

¼ cup oil
½ cup honey
2 eggs
juice of one lemon
grated rind of two lemons
1 cup whole wheat flour
¼ cup soy flour (you can substitute white flour if you don't have any soy)
2 tbsp. dried milk
2 tbsp. baking powder
½ cup sesame seeds
juice of one lemon (for topping)
3 tbsp. honey

1. Beat oil and honey until blended.
2. Stir in eggs, lemon juice and grated rind.
3. Mix all dry ingredients and sesame seeds and then stir them into the honey mixture.
4. Bake in a small oiled loaf pan (preferably smaller than 5x9) at 350 degrees for 45 minutes.
5. Combine lemon juice and honey.
6. Poke holes in cake and pour topping over it while it's still warm.
7. Cool for 10 minutes and then remove from pan.

I used to use Bisquick quite a lot for making biscuits, pancakes, waffles, and shortbread. When I finally read the label one day, I found that it was preserved with BHA and BHT and used hydrogenated oils beside. So I now make my own and store it in a jar and use it as I would the commerical brand.

a better biscuit mix *

3 cups flour
1 tsp. salt
¼ tsp. cream of tartar
1½ tbsp. baking powder
⅔ cups shortening

1. Mix all dry ingredients.
2. Cut in shortening until mix is crumbly.
3. Store in refrigerator and use as a base for biscuits, waffles, pancakes, shortbread, and coffeecake.

Walnut bread is an easy recipe and good to have for breakfast in the morning. If you have already made your biscuit mix and have it on hand, it takes about 2 minutes to prepare.

walnut bread *

1 egg, beaten
¾ cup milk
½ cup sugar
3 cups biscuit mix
1 tbsp. grated orange peel
1 cup chopped walnuts

1. Stir egg, milk, sugar and biscuit mix.
2. Add grated peel and walnuts.
3. Pour into a greased loaf pan and bake at 350 degrees for about 1 hour.

I get discouraged trying to find breakfast coffee cakes and muffins in the supermarket that are not made with preservatives, artificial coloring and artificial flavors and I also get tired of the usual toast each morning. So, I was happy to be given a nice, easy recipe for pumpkin muffins by Judy Wolfe. I usually make a batch and freeze some of them to be used later.

judy's pumpkin muffins *

1½ cups white flour, sifted
2 tsp. baking powder, sifted
½ cup brown sugar
½ tsp. salt
½ tsp. cinnamon
½ tsp. nutmeg
½ cup unsweetened pumpkin
1 egg
¼ cup melted butter
½ cup raisins
¼ cup sugar

1. Mix all ingredients. Batter may be a little lumpy.
2. Pour batter into 12 greased medium sized muffin cups.
3. Sprinkle a little sugar over the top of each muffin.
4. Bake in a pre-heated oven of 400 degrees for 18 to 20 minutes.

southern chili cornbread *

bacon drippings or butter
2 cups yellow cornmeal
1½ cups flour
1 tsp. sugar
1 tsp. salt
2½ tsp. baking powder
1 egg, beaten
4 tbsp. melted butter
1 tbsp. safflower oil
2 cups milk (jpreferably skim milk)
⅓ cup green chilis, cut in small pieces

1. Place bacon drippings or butter in large, heavy skillet and put in 400 degree oven to melt.
2. Sift all dry ingredients in bowl.
3. Add beaten egg, melted butter, safflower oil and mix.
4. Stir in milk and chili pieces and mix well.
5. Place in hot skillet in oven and cook for 45 minutes or until the top is nicely browned.

mother's zucchini bread *

2 cups zucchini, grated
3 eggs, beaten
1 cup safflower oil
2 cups sugar
3 tsp. vanilla
3 cups flour
1 tsp. baking soda
¼ tsp. baking powder
1 tsp. salt
3 tsp. cinnamon
½ cup chopped walnuts

1. In a bowl, lightly mix zucchini, eggs, oil and sugar.
2. In another bowl, mix all the rest of the ingredients.
3. Combine all ingredients and pour into two lightly greased loaf pans.
4. Bake at 350 degree for approximately 1 hour and 15 minutes or until a toothpick comes out clean.

I can't tell you how many times people have said to me that Rosalie Gwathmey is the best cook in the Hamptons. The wife of a painter, the mother of an architect, Rosalie is an artist in her own right and she is also an artist in the kitchen. When I asked her if she would like to give me a recipe, she said she didn't know why people didn't make batterbread any more. Now we will. There is another thing about Rosalie, she has a beautiful smile, her whole face lights up.

rosalie gwathmey's batterbread *

½ cup cornmeal
1½ cups milk
4 tbsp. butter
4 eggs at room temperature
1 tsp. salt

1. Cook cornmeal and milk in a saucepan stirring constantly until thick. Set aside.
2. Heat oven to 375 degrees. Put butter in a 2-qt. casserole and melt in oven.
3. Separate eggs and beat the yolks into the cornmeal mixture.
4. Pour into the casserole and mix with the butter.
5. Sprinkle salt over the egg whites and beat into soft peaks.
6. Add a little of the egg whites to the batter and stir.
7. Fold the rest of the whites into the batter.
8. Bake about 40 minutes or until golden.

sandwiches

This is just a list, not recipes, but if you're like me and never know what to make for lunch, it might come in handy. I actually like leftovers for lunch, but they're not always available. Then, I'm in a quandry. I don't care for coldcuts and I get very tired of the standard tuna and egg salad. I decided to make a list of sandwiches, so I wouldn't waste my time trying to always figure out what to have for lunch. I hope by listing the ingredients, they will be easy to follow. Needless to say, good bread is a must.

1. Pocket veggies — pita bread with raw zucchini slices, alfalfa sprouts, shreds of purple cabbage, carrots, celery, and Swiss cheese put in oven wrapped in foil until cheese melts.
2. Pita bread filled with tahini, tomatoes, onions, sprouts and avocado.
3. A breakfast pita sandwich — pita filled with apple slices and tahini.
4. Pita bread filled with cottage cheese, scallions, radishes, cucumber, celery and sprinkled with celery salt.
5. Cream cheese mixed with chopped scallions, sprouts, watercress and sprinkled with thyme.
6. Cream cheese, sliced olives and alfalfa sprouts on whole wheat.
7. Cream cheese, chopped olives, scallions and pimento on black bread.
8. Bagels with cream cheese, lox, tomatoes and onions.
9. My mother-in-law's invention — bagels, cream cheese, tomatoes, onions and sliced, black olives.
10. Bacon, cream cheese and red onion.
11. Open faced sandwich — onion, tomato, Montery jack and green chilis, broiled.
12. Grilled cheese — always with pickles on the side.
13. Grilled cheese with bacon.
14. Open faced grilled cheese with tomato slices and onion.
15. Ham and Swiss cheese with mayonnaise and butter, grilled like a regular grilled cheese sandwich.
16. Broiled open faced sandwich with Swiss cheese and apple on rye.
17. Open faced sandwich with Camenbert cheese, sliced ham and tomato on whole wheat.
18. Mozzarella cheese and anchovy pieces on Italian bread, placed under broiler until cheese melts.
19. Mortadella, provolone and marinated red peppers on Italian bread.
20. Cottage cheese, tomato, cucumber and onion on rye.
21. Cheese, green chilis and scallions on whole wheat bread.
22. Grilled tomato and onion slices with crumbled tofu.
23. Avocado, tomato, chopped scallions and Russian dressing on whole wheat.
24. Peanut butter and sliced bananas on toasted whole wheat.
25. Egg salad with onions, celery, and minced carrots.
26. Rhoda's tofu salad (see chapter on salads).
27. Bacon and egg.

28. Bacon, lettuce and tomato.
29. My Father's favorite — bacon and avocado.
30. Club sandwiches, bacon, lettuce, tomato, and sliced chicken with mayonnaise.
31. Bacon and chicken salad.
32. Roast beef on rye with sliced, cooked beets and horseradish sauce.
33. Roast beef with red onion, lettuce and mayonnaise mixed with mustard and horseradish sauce on pumpernickel.
34. Cornbeef on rye with Swiss cheese, sauerkraut, Dijon mustard and Russian dressing.
35. Tuna, diced cooked potatoes, chickpeas and onions mixed with mayonnaise.
36. Tuna, tiny diced carrots, onions, and olives with mayonnaise.
37. Canned salmon mixed with mayonnaise and asparagus, tomato and cucumber on rye or cornbread.
38. Canned salmon with mayonnaise and dill, lettuce and cucumber on toast.

good and useful cookbooks

The Natural Foods Cookbook by Beatrice Trum Hunter
The Supermarket Cookbook by Nikki and David Goldbeck
Yoga Natural Foods Cookbook by Richard Hittleman
Whole Grain Cookery by Stella Standard
Soups For All Seasons by Stella Standard
Future Food by Colin Tudge
Great Bread by Bernice Hunt
Vegetarian Epicure by Anna Thomas
World of the East-Vegetarian Cooking by Madhur Jaffrey
Moosewood Cookbook Mollie Katsen
Diet For A Small Planet by Frances Moore Lappe
Recipes For A Small Planet by Ellen Buchman Ewald

Index

notes

notes

notes

notes